EX LIBRIS

VINTAGE CLASSICS

A GUIDE FOR THE PERPLEXED

Before the publication of *Small is Beautiful*, his best-selling reappraisal of Western economic attitudes, Dr E. F. Schumacher was already well known as an economist, journalist and progressive entrepreneur. He was Economic Adviser to the National Coal Board from 1950 to 1970, and was also the originator of the concept of Intermediate Technology for developing countries and Founder and Chairman of the Intermediate Technology Development Group Ltd (now called Practical Action). He also served as President of the Soil Association (Britain's largest organic farming organisation, founded in 1946) and as Director of the Scott-Bader Company (pathfinders in polymer chemistry and common ownership).

Born in Germany, he first came to England in 1930 as a Rhodes Scholar to study economics at New College, Oxford. Later, at the age of twenty-two, he taught economics at Columbia University, New York. As he found theorising without practical experience unsatisfying, he then went into business, farming and journalism. He resumed the academic life for a period at Oxford during the war, afterwards serving as Economic Adviser to the British Control Commission in Germany from 1946 to 1950. In later years, his advice on problems of rural development was sought by many overseas governments.

Dr Schumacher was awarded the CBE in 1974. He died in 1977.

ALSO BY E. F. SCHUMACHER

Small is Beautiful
The Age of Plenty
Good Work

E. F. SCHUMACHER

A Guide for the Perplexed

WITHDRAWN

VINTAGE BOOKS
London

Published by Vintage 2011

6 8 10 9 7

First published in 1977 by Jonathan Cape
First published in Vintage 1995

Vintage
Random House, 20 Vauxhall Bridge Road,
London SW1V 2SA

www.vintage-classics.info

Addresses for companies within The Random House Group
Limited can be found at:
www.randomhouse.co.uk/offices.htm

The Random House Group Limited Reg. No. 954009

A CIP catalogue record for this book
is available from the British Library

ISBN 9780099480211

The Random House Group Limited supports The Forest Stewardship Council
(FSC®), the leading international forest certification organisation. Our books
carrying the FSC label are printed on FSC® certified paper. FSC is the only forest
certification scheme endorsed by the leading environmental organisations,
including Greenpeace. Our paper procurement policy can be found at
www.randomhouse.co.uk/environment

Printed and bound by
CPI Group (UK) Ltd, Croydon, CR0 4YY

Nulla est homini causa philosophandi,
nisi ut beatus sit
(St Augustine)

Man has no reason to philosophise
except with a view to happiness

Contents

Introduction

Five days before he died, Schumacher handed the finished manuscript of this book to his daughter with the words 'this is what my life has been leading up to'. Schumacher was one of the most brilliant thinkers of his day and unique in addressing *all* aspects of life and how they relate to each other in our world today, including how we should practically respond to it on an individual level and achieve balance. In our increasingly troubled world his words are even more relevant now than in his lifetime and applying his insights can lead to extraordinary levels of health and happiness, rather than chasing consumptive and illusory comforts.

Our biggest problems often occur when we get the simplest, most subtle but important things wrong. This book is nothing short of a *guide for life*, in that it both explains the pitfalls of many debased current cultural and societal influences, such as relying only on what we can prove through materialistic science, but even more importantly, the book describes the benefits of accessing and developing our higher consciousness powers to our own and society's advantage. This equates to something of a 'missing link' in today's society and explains many of the problems we are not able to deal with by current thinking. With balanced consciousness across our physical, social and personal transformative needs our consumptive behaviours will also become sustainable. I call this desired state 'full spectrum consciousness', a phrase well understood by the businesses and organisations I have pioneered this work with over many decades.

On reading *A Guide for the Perplexed* several things may strike you. Firstly, the structural ideas, models and 'great truths' it presents are underpinned by an extremely broad understanding of a wide range of ancient and modern thinkers, fully referenced from all of recorded history. Schumacher is regarded as being in the vanguard of the holistic thinking that occurred in the 1960s and 1970s, although he would say he was not coming up with anything new. The reality he expresses is ageless and beautiful in that it extracts just the salient, simple things we need to know. Schumacher is not selling a way of thinking but reflecting a way of being we each have to understand for ourselves.

Secondly, Schumacher explains where things have gone wrong in human consciousness development, or more truthfully society's deviation from it the last few hundred years, instead chasing *false gods*, with examples from Descartes to modern Scientism and personal consumptive meeting of desires. He illustrates the unbalanced limited thinking much of our modern culture has accumulated and the short term *cul-de-sacs* we have rushed into in the last fifty years and encourages us back on track. Unfortunately, his words have not been widely heeded and so, with a burgeoning population and widening economic expectations worldwide, these messages are even more relevant today – but with a bigger gap to bridge. The clarity with which these explanations are expressed not only makes them accessible, but gives them a gravitas that quickens the core of the curious, thinking man[1] looking for simplicity, truth and happiness. Schumacher guides us to understanding how our mainstream culture and media bias is now quite out of sorts with reality, thus leading to the big problems we have today.

The third great and joyful aspect of this book is that Schumacher defines a cosmology and ways of being that explain

---

[1] I use Schumacher's parlance here of man to represent all humanity, each member of which he considered equal, worthy and important in what they thought and did.

how we can escape our un-spirited darkness by combining ancient wisdoms and modern thinking. He is able to turn the top level perspective into personal level thinking and actions to help us lead ourselves into more fulfilling lives that reflect our purpose here on earth. Schumacher remarkably bridges the gap between old faiths, new age and Scientism thinking that makes him as relevant today as he was in the 1970s. He is positive that the ills of our current world can be solved, but that this needs dedication to personal reflection and better, higher levels of awareness through experience and self-discipline that he outlines. One personally challenging truth is that it is only through individual personal commitment multiplied many times that we can solve these problems.

One might be overawed by the problems and solutions outlined, but experience in coming to terms with problems in various modern organisations reflects the positive picture Schumacher portrays. Increasing consultant and guru analysis on what stops organisations from delivering better performance identifies similar things to Schumacher: namely that poor understanding by leaders about themselves and the way they communicate alienates people below them, creating 'blocks' in the deeper consciousness. Critical issues often seem to be avoided because people do not have the understanding, language or structure to face them. This inevitably leads to low morale, independent non-aligned thought and discontinuities in actions because of too limited a perspective. The good news is that various tools are being developed to bridge this gap for businesses based on fundamental values that are being compromised. Removing these 'blocks' allows more people to contribute to the organisation in aligned ways that brings gains to all in business performance and employee satisfaction. In this book, Schumacher provides us with the guide to doing this for our own lives with our own choice of route.

We should feel positive that Schumacher says *nothing* in the book that is beyond each and every one of us, in fact most of the answers are simple if we approach them at the right level and also include our intuitive senses. Schumacher guides us as to which problems usefully succumb to hard fact science (Convergent problems) and which need us to listen to our higher values (balanced from contemplating the Four Fields of Knowledge).

It is clear to me that the degree of perplexity we experience as humans and our ability to cope with our problems is directly correlated with our ability to become empathetic to our own intuitive 'sixth sense' nature (suppressing the purely selfish and finding the heart) and the nature of the human collective. This is a quiet voice that needs to be nurtured in a noisy world. We see the world not as it is, but through the lens of the beliefs, values and assumptions that we cling to in defining who we are. The source of our perplexity is ultimately not in the problems we face but within ourselves. As we evolve in our self-knowledge, we also evolve in our knowledge of others. Our ability to manipulate our world has evolved out of balance with our beliefs, values and our ethical relationship to the world. What we identify with we care for. Schumacher appeals to us to travel the inner journey through everyday reflection. Through being wiser and healed individuals internally we shall naturally heal the earth externally too.

Richard Barrett
Chairman, Barrett Values Centre
May 2011

Postscript – I would like to express my thanks to Diana Schumacher, Barbara Wood, Nicola Schumacher and Peter Bruce for their help in understanding the nature of Fritz Schumacher's thinking in writing this introduction.

Richard Barrett is founder and Chairman of the Barrett Values Centre and is an internationally recognised author, speaker and consultant on leadership, values and culture in business and society. He has pioneered practical work very much in keeping with Schumacher's principles developing Values Mapping and Cultural Change Transformation Toolsets, a Full Spectrum Consciousness and values-based Leadership models that supports his work with organisational leaders in the public and private sector to remove their inefficiencies, improve alignment to core values and raise their consciousness awareness and operating level.

He is a visiting lecturer at the Consulting and Coaching for Change leadership course run jointly by HEC Executive Education in Paris and the Saïd Business School, University of Oxford. He is also an adjunct professor at Royal Roads University, Institute for Values-based Leadership in Canada.

His books include:

A Guide to Liberating Your Soul (1995)

Liberating the Corporate Soul:
Building a Visionary Organization (1998)

Building a Values-Driven Organization: A Whole System
Approach to Cultural Transformation (2006)

The New Leadership Paradigm (2010)

Acknowledgments

The author and publisher wish to acknowledge permission to quote from E. Gilson, *The Unity of Philosophical Experience* (Sheed and Ward); from two books by Maurice Nicoll, *Living Time and the Integration of the Life* and *Psychological Commentaries on the Teaching of Gurdjieff and Ouspensky*, vol. I, both published by Watkins Publishing House; W. T. Stace, *Mysticism and Philosophy* (Macmillan, London and Basingstoke); G. N. M. Tyrrell, *Grades of Significance* (Hutchinson); and from Whitall N. Perry, *A Treasury of Traditional Wisdom*, published by George Allen and Unwin.

I

On Philosophical Maps

I

On a visit to Leningrad some years ago[1] I consulted a map to find out where I was, but I could not make it out. I could see several enormous churches, yet there was no trace of them on my map. When finally an interpreter came to help me, he said: 'We don't show churches on our maps.' Contradicting him, I pointed to one that was very clearly marked. 'This is a museum,' he said, 'not what we call a "living church". It is only the "living churches" we don't show.'

It then occurred to me that this was not the first time I had been given a map that failed to show many of the things I could see right in front of my eyes. All through school and university I had been given maps of life and knowledge on which there was hardly a trace of many of the things that I most cared about and that seemed to me to be of the greatest possible importance for the conduct of my life. I remembered that for many years my perplexity was complete; and no interpreter came along to help me. It remained complete until I ceased to suspect the sanity of my perceptions and began, instead, to suspect the soundness of the maps.

The maps I was given advised me that virtually all my ancestors, until a quite recent generation, had been rather pathetic illusionists who conducted their lives on the basis of irrational beliefs and absurd superstitions. Even illustrious scientists like Johann Kepler or Isaac Newton apparently had spent most of their time and energy on nonsensical studies of non-existing things. Throughout history, enormous amounts of hard-earned wealth were squandered to the honour and glory of imaginary deities—not only by my European forebears, but by all peoples, in all parts of the world, at all times. Everywhere thousands of seemingly healthy men and women subjected themselves to utterly meaningless restrictions, like voluntary fasting; tormented themselves by celibacy; wasted their time on pilgrimages, fantastic rituals, repetitive prayers, and so forth; turning their backs on reality—and some actually still do it even in this enlightened age!—all for nothing, all out of ignorance and stupidity; none of it to be taken seriously today, except of course as museum pieces. What a history of error from which we had emerged! What a history of taking for real what every modern child knew to be totally unreal and imaginary! Our entire past, except the most recent, was today fit only for museums where people could satisfy their curiosity about the oddity and incompetence of earlier generations. What our ancestors had written was also in the main fit only for storage in libraries where historians and other specialists could study these relics and write books about them. Knowledge of the past was considered interesting and occasionally thrilling but of no particular value for learning to cope with the problems of the present.

All this and many other things of a similar kind I was taught at school and university, although not in so many words, not plainly and frankly. It would not do to call a spade a spade—ancestors had to be treated with respect; they could not help their backwardness; they tried hard and sometimes even got quite near the truth in a haphazard sort of way. Their preoccupation with religion was just one of their many signs of underdevelopment, not surprising with people who had not yet come of age. There was, of course, some interest in religion even today which legitimised that of earlier times. It was still permissible, on suitable occasions, to refer to God the Creator, although every educated person knew that there was not really a God, certainly not one capable of creating anything, and that the things around us had come into existence by a process of mindless evolution, that is by chance and natural selection. Our ancestors, unfortunately, did not know about evolution, and so they invented all these fanciful myths.

The maps of *real* knowledge, designed for *real* life, did not show anything except things that allegedly could be *proved* to exist. The first principle of the philosophical map-makers seemed to be 'If in doubt, leave it out', or put it into a museum. It occurred to me, however, that the question of what constitutes proof was a very subtle and difficult one. Would it not be wiser to turn the principle into its opposite and say 'If in doubt, show it *prominently*'? After all, matters that are beyond doubt are, in a sense, dead; they do not constitute a challenge to the living.

To accept anything as true means to incur the risk of error. If I limit myself to knowledge that I consider true beyond doubt, I minimise the risk of error but I maximise, at the same time, the risk of missing out on what may be the subtlest, most important and most rewarding things in life. St Thomas Aquinas, following Aristotle, taught that 'the slenderest knowledge that may be obtained of the highest things is more desirable than the most certain knowledge obtained of lesser things.'² 'Slender' knowledge is here put in opposition to 'certain' knowledge, and indicates uncertainty. Maybe it is necessarily so that the higher things cannot be known with the same degree of certainty as the lesser things can be known, in which case it would be a very great loss indeed if knowledge were limited to things beyond the possibility of doubt.

The philosophical maps with which I was supplied at school and university did not merely fail to show 'living churches', like the map of Leningrad to which I have referred; they also failed to show large 'unorthodox' sections of both theory and practice in medicine, agriculture, psychology and the social and political sciences, not to mention art and so-called occult or paranormal phenomena, the mere mention of which was considered to be a sign of mental deficiency. In particular, all the most prominent doctrines shown on the 'map' accepted the possibility of art only as self-expression or escape from reality. Even in nature there was nothing artistic except by chance; that is to say, even the most beautiful appearances could be fully accounted for—so we were told—by their utility for reproduction, affecting natural selection. In fact, apart from 'museums', the entire map from right to left and from top to bottom was drawn in utilitarian colours: hardly anything was shown as existing unless it could be interpreted as profitable for man's comfort or useful in the universal battle for survival.

Not surprisingly, the more thoroughly we became acquainted with the details of the map—the more we absorbed what it showed and got used to the absence of the things it did not show—the more perplexed, unhappy and cynical we became. Some of us, however, had experiences similar to that described by the late Dr Maurice Nicoll:

> Once, in the Greek New Testament class on Sundays, taken by the Head Master, I dared to ask, in spite of my stammering, what some parable meant. The answer was so confused that I actually experienced my first moment of consciousness—that is, I suddenly realised that *no one knew anything* ... and from that moment I began to think for myself, or rather knew that I could ... I remember so clearly this class-room, the high windows constructed so that we could not see out of them, the desks, the platform on which the Head Master sat, his scholarly, thin face, his nervous habits of twitching his mouth and jerking his hands—and suddenly this inner revelation of *knowing that he knew nothing*—nothing that is, about anything that really mattered. This was my first inner liberation from the power of external life. From that time, I knew for certain— and that means always by inner individual authentic perception which is the only source of real knowledge— that all my loathing of religion as it was taught me was right.[3]

The maps produced by modern materialistic scientism leave all the questions that really matter unanswered. More than that, they do not even show a way to a possible answer: they deny the validity of the questions. The situation was desperate enough in my youth half a century ago; it is even worse now because the ever more rigorous application of the scientific method to all subjects and disciplines has destroyed even the last remnants of ancient wisdom—at least in the Western world. It is being loudly proclaimed, in the name of scientific objectivity, that 'values and meanings are nothing but defence mechanisms and reaction formations';[4] that man is 'nothing but a complex biochemical mechanism powered by a combustion system which energises computers with prodigious storage facilities for retaining encoded information';[5] Sigmund

Freud even assured us that 'this alone I know with certainty, namely that man's value judgments are guided absolutely by their desire for happiness, and are therefore merely an attempt to bolster up their illusions by arguments.'[6]

How is anyone to resist the pressure of such statements, made in the name of objective science, unless, like Maurice Nicoll, he suddenly receives 'this inner revelation' of knowing that men, however learned they might be, who say such things, *know nothing about anything that really matters*? People are asking for bread and they are being given stones. They beg for advice about what they should do 'to be saved', and they are told that the idea of salvation has no intelligible content and is nothing but an infantile neurosis. They long for guidance on how to live as responsible human beings, and they are told that they are machines, like computers, without free will and therefore without responsibility.

'The present danger', says Dr Viktor E. Frankl, a psychiatrist of unshakeable sanity, 'does not really lie in the loss of universality on the part of the scientist, but rather in his pretence and claim of totality ... What we have to deplore therefore is not so much the fact that *scientists are specialising*, but rather the fact that *specialists are generalising*.' After many centuries of theological imperialism, we have now had three centuries of an ever more aggressive 'scientific imperialism', and the result is a degree of bewilderment and disorientation, particularly among the young, which can at any moment lead to the collapse of our civilisation. 'The true nihilism of today', says Dr Frankl, 'is reductionism ... Contemporary nihilism no longer brandishes the word nothingness; today nihilism is camouflaged as *nothing-but-ness*. Human phenomena are thus turned into mere epiphenomena.'[7]

Yet they remain our *reality*, everything we are and everything we become. In this life we find ourselves as in a strange country. Ortega y Gasset once remarked that 'life is fired at us point-blank'. We cannot say: 'Hold it! I am not quite ready. Wait until I have sorted things out.' Decisions have to be taken that we are not ready for; aims have to be chosen that we cannot see clearly. This is very strange and, on the face of it, quite irrational. Human beings, it seems, are insufficiently 'programmed'. Not only are they utterly helpless when they are born and remain so for a long time: even when fully grown they do not move and act with the surefootedness of animals. They hesitate, doubt, change their minds, run hither and thither, uncertain not simply of how to get what they want, but above all of what they want.

Questions like 'What should I do?' or 'What must I do to be saved?' are strange questions because they relate to *ends*, not simply to means. No technical answer will do, such as 'Tell me precisely what you want and I shall tell you how to get it.' The whole point is that I do not know what I want. Maybe all I want is to be happy. But the answer, 'Tell me what you need for happiness, and I shall then be able to advise you what to do'—this answer, again, will not do, because I do not know what I need for happiness. Perhaps someone says: 'For happiness you need wisdom'—but what is wisdom? 'For happiness you need the truth that makes you free'—but what is the truth that makes us free? Who will tell me where I can find it? Who can guide me to it or at least point out the direction in which I have to proceed?

In this book, we shall look at the world and try and see it whole. To do this is sometimes called to philosophise, and philosophy has been defined as the love of, and seeking after, wisdom. Socrates said: 'Wonder is the feeling of a philosopher, and philosophy begins with wonder.' He also said: 'No god is a philosopher or seeker after wisdom for he is wise already. Neither do the ignorant seek after wisdom; for herein is the evil of ignorance, that he who is neither good nor wise is nevertheless satisfied with himself.'[8]

One way of looking at the world as a whole is by means of a map, that is to say, some sort of a plan or outline that shows where the various things are to be found—not all things, of course, for that would make the map as big as the world, but the things that are most prominent, most important for orientation: outstanding landmarks, as it were, which you cannot miss or which, if you do miss them, leave you in total perplexity. The most important part of any inquiry or exploration is its beginning. As has often been pointed out, if a false or superficial beginning has been made, one may employ the most rigorous methods during the later stages of investigation but they will never retrieve the situation.[9]

Map-making is an empirical art which makes use of a high degree of abstraction but none the less clings to reality with something akin to self-abandonment. Its motto, in a sense, is 'Accept everything; reject nothing.' If something is *there*, if it has any kind of existence, if people notice it and are interested in it, it must be indicated on the map, in its proper place. Map-making is not the whole of philosophy, just as a map or guidebook is not the whole of geography. It is simply a beginning—the very beginning that is at present lacking, when people ask: 'What does it all mean?' or 'What am I supposed to do with my life?'

My map or guidebook is constructed on the recognition of four Great Truths—landmarks, as it were—which are so prominent, so all-pervading, that you can see them wherever you happen to be; and if you know them well, you can always find your location by them, and if you cannot recognise them, you are lost.

The guidebook, it might be said, is about 'Man lives in the world'. This simple statement indicates that we shall need to study

1 'The World';
2 'Man'—his equipment wherewith to meet 'the World';
3 his way of learning about the world; and
4 what it means to 'live' in this world.

The Great Truth about the world is that it is a hierarchical structure of at least four great Levels of Being.

The Great Truth about man's equipment wherewith to meet the world is the principle of 'adequateness' (*adaequatio*).

The Great Truth about man's learning relates to the 'Four Fields of Knowledge'.

The Great Truth about living this life, living in this world, relates to the distinction between two types of problem, 'convergent' and 'divergent'.

A map or guidebook, let this be understood as clearly as possible, does not 'solve' problems and does not 'explain' mysteries; it merely helps to identify them. Thereafter, everybody's task is as defined by the last words spoken by the Buddha: 'Work out your salvation with diligence.' For this purpose, according to the precepts of the Tibetan teachers,

a philosophy comprehensive enough to embrace the whole
of knowledge is indispensable;

a system of meditation which will produce the power of
concentrating the mind on anything whatsoever is
indispensable;

an art of living which will enable one to utilise each
activity (of body, speech and mind) as an aid on the Path
is indispensable.[10]

II

The more recent philosophers of Europe have seldom been
faithful map-makers. Descartes (1596–1650), for instance, to
whom modern philosophy owes so much, approached his self-
set task in quite a different way. 'Those who seek the direct
road to truth', he said, 'should not bother with any object of
which they cannot have a certainty equal to the demonstrations
of arithmetic and geometry.'[11] Only such objects should
engage our attention 'to the sure and indubitable knowledge
of which our mental powers seem to be adequate'.[12]

Descartes, the father of modern rationalism, insisted that 'we
should never allow ourselves to be persuaded excepting by the
evidence of our Reason', and he emphasised specially that he
spoke 'of our Reason and not of our imagination nor of our
senses'.[13] The method of reason is to 'reduce involved and
obscure propositions step by step to those that are simpler, and
then, starting with the intuitive apprehension of all those that
are absolutely simple, attempt to ascend to the knowledge of
all others by precisely similar steps'.[14] This is a programme
conceived by a mind both powerful and frighteningly narrow,
whose narrowness is further demonstrated by the Rule:

If in the matters to be examined we come to a step in
the series of which our understanding is not sufficiently
well able to have an intuitive cognition, we must stop
short there. We must make no attempt to examine
what follows; thus we shall spare ourselves superfluous
labour.[15]

Descartes limits his interest to knowledge and ideas that are
precise and certain beyond any possibility of doubt, because

his primary interest is that we should become 'masters and possessors of nature'. Nothing can be precise unless it can be quantified in one way or another. As Jacques Maritain comments,

> The mathematical knowledge of nature, for Descartes, is not what it is in reality, a certain interpretation of phenomena ... which does not answer questions bearing upon the first principles of things. This knowledge is, for him, the revelation of the very essence of things. These are analysed exhaustively by geometric extension and local movement. The whole of physics, that is, the whole of the philosophy of nature, is nothing but geometry.
>
> Thus Cartesian evidence goes straight to mechanism. It mechanises nature; it does violence to it; it annihilates everything which causes things to symbolise with the spirit, to partake of the genius of the Creator, to speak to us. The universe becomes dumb.[16]

There is no guarantee that the world is made in such a way that indubitable truth is the whole truth. And whose truth, whose understanding would it be? That of man. Of any man? Are all men 'adequate' to grasp all truth? As Descartes has demonstrated, the mind of man can doubt everything it cannot grasp with ease, and some men are more prone to doubt than others.

Descartes broke with tradition, made a clean sweep and undertook to start afresh, finding out everything by himself. This kind of arrogance became the 'style' of European philosophy. 'Every modern philosopher', as Maritain remarks, 'is a Cartesian in the sense that he looks upon himself as starting off in the absolute, and as having the mission of bringing men a new conception of the world.'[17]

The alleged fact that philosophy 'had been cultivated for many centuries by the best minds that have ever lived and that nevertheless no single thing is to be found in it which is not a subject of dispute and in consequence is not dubious'[18] led Descartes to what amounted to the 'withdrawal from wisdom' and the exclusive concentration on knowledge as firm and indubitable as mathematics and geometry. Francis Bacon (1561–1626) had already pleaded in a similar vein. Scepticism, a form of defeatism in philosophy, became the main current of European philosophy, which insisted, not without plausibility, that the reach of the human mind was strictly limited and that there was no point in taking any interest in matters beyond its capacity. While traditional wisdom had considered the human mind as weak but *open-ended*, that is capable of reaching beyond itself towards higher and higher levels, the new thinking took it as axiomatic that the mind's reach had fixed and narrow limits, which could be clearly determined, while within these limits it possessed virtually unlimited powers.

From the point of view of philosophical map-making, this meant a very great impoverishment: entire regions of human interest, which had engaged the most intense efforts of earlier generations, simply ceased to appear on the map. But there was also an even more significant withdrawal and impoverishment: while traditional wisdom had always presented the world as a three-dimensional structure (as symbolised by the cross), where it was not only meaningful but of essential importance to distinguish always and everywhere between 'higher' and 'lower' things and Levels of Being, the new thinking strove with determination, not to say fanaticism, to get rid of the *vertical dimension*. How could one obtain clear and precise ideas about such qualitative notions as 'higher' or 'lower'? Was it not the most urgent task of reason to put into their place quantitative measurements?

Perhaps the 'mathematicism' of Descartes had gone too far; so Immanuel Kant (1724–1804) set out to make a new start. But as Etienne Gilson, the incomparable master of the history of philosophy, remarks,

> Kant was not shifting from mathematics to philosophy, but from mathematics to physics. As Kant himself immediately concluded: 'The true method of metaphysics is fundamentally the same as that which Newton has introduced into natural science, and which has there yielded such fruitful results ...' *The Critique of Pure Reason* is a masterly description of what the structure of the human mind should be, in order to account for the existence of a Newtonian conception of nature, and assuming that

conception to be true to reality. Nothing can show more clearly the essential weakness of physicism as a philosophical method.[19]

Neither mathematics nor physics can entertain the qualitative notion of 'higher' or 'lower'. So the vertical dimension disappeared from the philosophical maps, which henceforth concentrated on somewhat far-fetched problems like 'Do other people exist?' or 'How can I know anything at all?' or 'Do other people have experiences analogous to mine?' and thus ceased to be of any help to people in the awesome task of picking their way through life.

The proper task of philosophy was formulated by Etienne Gilson as follows:

It is its permanent duty to order and to regulate an ever wider area of scientific knowledge, and to judge ever more complex problems of human conduct; it is its never-ended task to keep the old sciences in their natural limits, to assign their places, and their limits, to new sciences; last, not least, to keep all human activities, however changing their circumstances, under the sway of the same reason by which alone man remains the judge of his own works and, after God, the master of his own destiny.[20]

III

The loss of the vertical dimension meant that it was no longer possible to give an answer, other than a utilitarian one, to the question, 'What am I to do with my life?' The answer could be more individualistic-selfish or more social-unselfish, but it could not help being utilitarian: either 'Make yourself as comfortable as you can' or 'Work for the greatest happiness of the greatest number.' Nor was it possible to define the nature of man other than as that of an animal. A 'higher' animal? Yes, perhaps, but only in some respects; in many other respects many animals could be described as 'higher' than man, and so it would be best to try and avoid nebulous terms like 'higher' or 'lower', unless one spoke in strictly evolutionary terms. In the context of evolution, 'higher' could be generally associated with 'later', and man was undoubtedly a latecomer and could therefore be thought of as standing at the top of the evolutionary ladder.

None of this leads to a helpful answer to the question, 'What am I to do with my life?' Pascal had said: 'Man wishes to be happy and only exists to be happy and cannot wish not to be happy,'[21] but the new thinking of the philosophers insisted, with Kant, that 'he never can say definitely and consistently what it is that he really wishes' and he cannot 'determine with certainty what would make him truly happy; because to do so he would need to be omniscient.'[22] Traditional wisdom had a reassuringly plain answer: Man's happiness is to move *higher*, to develop his *highest* faculties, to gain knowledge of the *higher* and *highest* things and, if possible, to 'see God'. If he moves *lower*, develops only his *lower* faculties, which he shares with the animals, then he makes himself deeply unhappy, even to the point of despair.

With unperturbable certainty St Thomas Aquinas argued:

No man tends to do a thing by his desire and endeavour unless it be previously known to him. Wherefore since man is directed by divine providence *to a higher good than human frailty can attain* in the present life ... it was necessary for his mind to be bidden to *something higher* than those things to which our reason can reach in the present life, *so that he might learn to aspire*, and by his endeavours to tend to *something surpassing the whole state of the present life* ... It was with this motive that the philosophers, in order to wean men from sensible pleasures to virtue, took care to show that there are other goods of greater account than those which appeal to the senses, the taste of which things affords much greater delight to those who devote themselves to active or contemplative virtues.[23]

These teachings, which are the traditional wisdom of all peoples in all parts of the world, have become virtually incomprehensible to modern man, although he, too, desires nothing more than somehow to be able to rise above 'the whole state of the present life'. He hopes to do so by growing rich, by moving around at ever increasing speed, by travelling to the moon and into space. It is worth listening again to St Thomas:

> There is a desire in man, common to him and other animals, namely the desire for *the enjoyment of pleasure*: and this men pursue especially by leading a voluptuous life, and through lack of moderation become intemperate and incontinent. Now in that vision [the divine vision] there is the most perfect pleasure, all the more perfect than sensuous pleasure as the intellect is above the senses; as the good in which we shall delight surpasses all sensible good, is more penetrating, and more continuously delightful; and as that pleasure is freer from all alloy of sorrow or trouble of anxiety ...
>
> In this life there is nothing so like this ultimate and perfect happiness as the life of those who contemplate the truth, as far as possible here below. Hence the philosophers who were unable to obtain full knowledge of that final beatitude, placed man's ultimate happiness in that contemplation which is possible during this life. For this reason too, Holy Writ commends the contemplative rather than other forms of life, when our Lord said (Luke X.42): *Mary hath chosen the better part*, namely the contemplation of truth, *which shall not be taken from her*. For contemplation of truth begins in this life, but will be consummated in the life to come: *while the active and civic life does not transcend the limits of this life.*[24]

Most modern readers will be reluctant to believe that perfect happiness is attainable by methods of which their modern world knows nothing. However, belief or disbelief is not the matter at issue here. The point is that without the qualitative concepts of 'higher' and 'lower' it is impossible to even think of guidelines for living that lead beyond individual or collective utilitarianism and selfishness.

The ability to see the Great Truth of the hierarchic structure of the world, which makes it possible to distinguish between higher and lower Levels of Being, is one of the indispensable conditions of understanding. Without it, it is not possible to find out where everything has its proper and legitimate place. Everything, everywhere, can be understood only when its Level of Being is fully taken into account. Many things are true at a low Level of Being and become absurd at a higher level, and of course vice versa.

We therefore now turn to a study of the hierarchical structure of the world.

2

Levels of Being

I

Our task is to look at the world and see it whole.

We see what our ancestors have always seen: a great 'Chain of Being' which seems to divide naturally into four sections— four 'kingdoms', as they used to be called—mineral, plant, animal and human. This 'was, in fact, until not much more than a century ago, probably the most widely familiar conception of the general *scheme* of things, of the constitutive pattern of the universe'.[1] The Chain of Being can be seen as extending downwards from the highest to the lowest, or it can be seen upwards from the lowest to the highest. The ancient view begins with the Divine and sees the downward Chain of Being as an increasing distance from the centre and a progressive loss of qualities. The modern view, largely influenced by the theory of evolution, tends to start from inanimate matter and consider man the last link of the chain, having evolved the widest range of useful qualities. For our purposes, the direction of looking—upwards, or downwards—is unimportant at this stage, and in line with modern habits of thought we shall start at the lowest level, the mineral kingdom, and consider the successive gain of qualities, or powers, as we move to the higher levels.

No one has any difficulty in recognising the astonishing and mysterious difference between a living plant and one that has died and has thus fallen to the lowest Level of Being, inanimate matter. What is this power that has been lost? We call it 'life'. Scientists tell us that we must not talk of a 'life force' because no such force has ever been found to exist; yet the *difference* exists. We could call it '*x*', indicating something that

25

is there to be noticed and studied but cannot be explained. If we call the mineral level 'm', we can call the plant level $m + x$. This factor x is obviously worthy of our closest attention, particularly since we are able to destroy it although it is completely outside our knowledge and ability to create it. Even if somebody could provide us with a recipe, a set of instructions, on how life could be created out of lifeless matter, the mysterious character of 'x' would remain, and we should never cease to marvel that something that could do nothing is now able to extract nourishment from its environment, grow and reproduce itself, 'true to form', as it were. There is nothing in the laws, concepts and formulae of physics and chemistry to explain or even only to describe such powers. 'x' is something quite new and additional, and the more deeply we contemplate it the clearer it becomes that here we are faced with what might be called an *ontological discontinuity* or, more simply, a jump in the Level of Being.

From plant to animal, there is a similar jump, a similar addition of powers, which enables the typical, fully developed animal to do things that are totally outside the range of possibilities of the typical, fully developed plant. These powers, again, are mysterious and, strictly speaking, nameless. We can refer to them by means of the letter 'y', which will be the safest course, because any word-label we might attach to them can lead people to think that this was not merely a hint but an adequate description. However, we cannot talk without words, and I shall therefore attach to these mysterious powers the label 'consciousness'. It is easy to recognise consciousness in a dog, a cat or a horse, if only because they can be knocked unconscious, a condition similar to that of a plant: the processes of life are continuing although the animal has lost its peculiar powers.

If the plant, in the terminology used above, can be called $m + x$, the animal has to be described as $m + x + y$. Again, the factor y is worthy of the closest attention; we are able to destroy but not to create it. Anything that we can destroy but are unable to make is, in a sense, sacred, and all our 'explanations' of it do not really explain anything. Again we can say that 'y' is something quite new and additional, when compared with the level 'plant' — an *ontological discontinuity*, a jump in the Level of Being.

Moving from the animal level to the human level, who would seriously deny that there are, again, additional powers? What precisely they are has become a matter of controversy in modern times; but the fact that man is able to do—and is doing—innumerable things that lie totally outside the range of possibilities of even the most highly developed animals cannot be disputed and has never been denied. Man has powers of life like the plant, powers of consciousness like the animal, and evidently something more: the mysterious power 'z'. What is it? How could it be defined? What could it be called? This power 'z' has undoubtedly a great deal to do with the fact that man is not only able to think but also able to be aware of his thinking. Consciousness and intelligence, as it were, recoil upon themselves. There is not merely a conscious being, but a being capable of being conscious of its consciousness; not merely a thinker, but a thinker capable of watching and studying his own thinking. There is something able to say 'I' and to direct consciousness in accordance with its own purposes; a master or controller, a power at a higher level than consciousness itself. This power 'z', consciousness recoiling upon itself, opens up unlimited possibilities of purposeful learning, investigating, exploring, formulating and accumulating knowledge. What shall we call it? As it is necessary to have word-labels, I shall call it 'self-awareness'. We must, however, take great care always to remember that such a word-label is merely (to use a Buddhist phrase) 'a finger pointing to the moon'. The 'moon' itself remains highly mysterious and needs to be studied with the greatest patience and perseverance, if we want to understand anything about man's position in the universe.

Our initial review of the four great Levels of Being can be summed up as follows.

'Man' can be written $m + x + y + z$

'Animal' can be written $m + x + y$

'Plant' can be written $m + x$

'Mineral' can be written m

x, y and z are invisible; only m is visible; they are extremely difficult to grasp, although their effects are matters of everyday experience.

As we have mentioned before, instead of taking 'minerals' as our base-line and reaching the higher Levels of Being by an addition of powers, we could start with the highest level directly known to us—man—and reach the lower Levels of Being by a progressive subtraction of powers. We could then say:

Man can be written M
Animal can be written $M-z$
Plant can be written $M-z-y$
Mineral can be written $M-z-y-x$.

Such a 'downward' scheme is easier for us to understand than the 'upward' one, simply because it can be based on practical experience. We know that all three factors—x, y and z—can weaken and die away; we can in fact deliberately destroy them. Self-awareness can disappear while consciousness continues; consciousness can disappear while life continues; and life can disappear leaving an inanimate body behind. We can observe and in a sense *feel* the process of diminution to the point of the apparently total disappearance of self-awareness, consciousness and life. But it is outside our power to give life to inanimate matter, to give consciousness to living matter, and finally to add the power of self-awareness to conscious beings.

What we can do ourselves, we can in a sense understand; what we cannot do at all, we cannot understand—not even 'in a sense'. Evolution as a process of the spontaneous, accidental emergence of the powers of life, consciousness and self-awareness, out of inanimate matter is utterly and totally incomprehensible. If the accidental emergence of the higher from the lower is possible, then anything and everything is possible, and there is no basis for human thought. Two plus two would not have to be four but could just as well be five or anything else; nor would there be any necessity for us to believe that two minus two leaves nothing: why not believe it could accidentally make five?

For our purposes, however, there is no need to enter into such speculations at this stage. We hold fast to what we can see and experience: the Universe as a great hierarchic structure of four markedly different Levels of Being. Each level is obviously a broad band, allowing for higher and lower beings within the band, and the precise determination of where the lower band ends and the higher band begins may sometimes be a matter of difficulty and dispute. The existence of the four kingdoms, however, is not put into question by the fact that some of the frontiers are occasionally disputed.

Physics and chemistry deal with the lowest level, 'mineral'. At this level, x, y and z—life, consciousness, and self-awareness —do not exist (or, in any case, are totally inoperative and therefore cannot be noticed.) Physics and chemistry can tell us nothing, absolutely nothing, about them. These sciences possess no concepts relating to such powers and are incapable of describing their effects. Where there is life there is form, Gestalt, which reproduces itself over and over again from seed or similar beginnings, which do not possess this Gestalt but develop it in the process of growth. Nothing comparable fits into the scheme of physics or chemistry.

To say that life is nothing but a property of certain peculiar combinations of atoms is like saying that Shakespeare's *Hamlet* is nothing but a property of a peculiar combination of letters. The truth is that the peculiar combination of letters is nothing but a property of Shakespeare's *Hamlet*. The French or German versions of the play 'own' different combinations of letters.

The extraordinary thing about the modern 'life sciences' is that they hardly ever deal with *life as such*, the factor x, but devote infinite attention to the study and analysis of the physico-chemical body that is life's carrier. It may well be that modern science has no method for coming to grips with 'life as such'. If this is so let it be frankly admitted; there is no excuse for the pretence that life is nothing but physics and chemistry.

Nor is there any excuse for the pretence that consciousness is nothing but a property of life. To describe an animal as a physico-chemical system of extreme complexity is no doubt perfectly correct, except that it misses out on the 'animalness' of the animal. Some zoologists, at least, have advanced beyond this level of erudite absurdity and have developed an ability to see animals as more than complex machines. Their influence, however, is as yet deplorably small, and with the increasing 'rationalisation' of the modern life-style more and more animals are being treated as if they really were nothing but 'animal machines'. (This is a very telling example of how philosophical theories, no matter how absurd and offensive to common sense, tend to become, after a while, 'normal practice' in everyday life.)

All the 'humanities', as distinct from the natural sciences, deal in one way or another with factor y—consciousness. But a distinction between consciousness (y) and self-awareness (z) is seldom drawn. As a result, modern thinking has become increasingly uncertain of whether or not there is any 'real' difference between animal and man. A great deal of study is being undertaken of the behaviour of animals for the purpose of understanding the nature of man. This is analogous to studying physics with the hope of learning something about *life* (x). Naturally, since man, as it were, contains the three lower Levels of Being, certain things about him can be elucidated by studying minerals, plants, and animals—in fact, everything can be learned about him except that which makes him human. All the four constituent elements of the human person—m, x, y and z—deserve study; but there can be little doubt about their relative importance in terms of knowledge for the conduct of our lives. This importance increases in the order given above, and so does the difficulty and uncertainty experienced by modern humanity. Is there really anything beyond the world of matter, of molecules and atoms and electrons and innumerable other small particles, the ever more complex combinations of which allegedly account for simply everything, from the crudest to the most sublime? Why talk about fundamental differences, 'jumps' in the Chain of Being or 'ontological discontinuities' when all we can be really sure of are *differences in degree*? It is not necessary for us to battle over the question of whether the palpable and overwhelmingly obvious differences between the four great Levels of Being are best seen as differences in kind or differences in degree. What has to be fully understood is that there are differences in kind, and not simply in degree, between the powers of life, consciousness and self-awareness. Maybe traces of these powers exist already at the lower levels, although not noticeable (or not yet noticed) by man. Or maybe they are infused, as it were, on appropriate occasions from 'another world'. It is not essential for us to have theories about their origin, provided we recognise their quality and, in recognising their quality, never fail to remember that they are beyond anything our own intelligence enables us to create.

It is not unduly difficult to appreciate the difference between

'alive' and 'lifeless'; it is more difficult to distinguish consciousness from life; to realise, experience and appreciate the
difference between self-awareness and consciousness (that is,
between y and z) is hard indeed. The reason for the difficulty is
not far to seek: while the higher comprises and therefore in a
sense understands the lower, no being can understand anything
higher than itself. A human being can indeed strain and
stretch towards the higher and induce a process of growth
through adoration, awe, wonder, admiration and imitation, and
by attaining a higher level expand its understanding—and this
is a subject that will occupy us extensively later on. But people
with whom the power of self-awareness (z) is poorly developed
cannot grasp it as a separate power and tend to take it as
nothing but a slight extension of consciousness (y). Hence we
are given a large number of definitions of man which make him
out to be nothing but an exceptionally intelligent animal with
an unduly large brain, or a tool-making animal, or a political
animal, or an unfinished animal, or simply a naked ape. No
doubt, people who use these terms cheerfully include themselves
in their definitions and will have some reason for doing so. For
others they sound merely inane, like defining a dog as a barking
plant or a running cabbage. Nothing is more conducive to
the brutalisation of the modern world than the launching, in
the name of science, of wrongful and degraded definitions of
man, such as 'the naked ape'. What could one expect of
such a creature, of other 'naked apes' or, indeed, of oneself?
When people speak of animals as 'animal machines' they soon
start treating them accordingly, and when they think of
people as naked apes, all doors are opened to the free entry of
bestiality.

'What a piece of work is a man! How noble in reason! How
infinite in faculty!' Because of the power of self-awareness (z),
his faculties are indeed infinite; they are not narrowly determined, confined, or 'programmed', as one says today. Werner
Jaeger expressed a profound truth in the statement that, once
a human potentiality is realised, it exists. The greatest human
achievements define man—not the common run, not any
average behaviour or performance, and certainly not anything
that can be derived from the observation of animals. 'All men
cannot be outstanding,' says Dr Catherine Roberts,

Yet all men, through knowledge of superior humanness, could know what it means to be a human being and that they too have a contribution to make. It is magnificent to become as human as one is able. And it requires no help from science. In addition, the very act of realising one's potentialities might constitute an advance over what has gone before.[2]

This 'open-endedness' is the wonderful result of the specifically human powers of self-awareness (z), which, as distinct from the powers of life and consciousness, have nothing automatic or mechanical about them. The powers of self-awareness are, essentially, a limitless potentiality rather than an actuality. They have to be developed and 'realised' by each human individual if he is to become truly human, that is to say, a *person*.

I said earlier on that man can be written

$$m + x + y + z.$$

These four elements form a sequence of increasing rarity and vulnerability. Matter (m) cannot be destroyed; to kill a body means to deprive it of x, y and z, but the inanimate matter remains; it 'returns' to the earth. Compared with inanimate matter, life is exceedingly rare and precarious; all the same, compared with the ubiquitousness and tenacity of life, consciousness is very rare and vulnerable. When it comes to self-awareness, that is the rarest power of all, precious and vulnerable to the highest degree, a supreme and generally fleeting achievement of a person, present at one moment and all too easily gone at the next. The study of this factor z has at all ages—except the present—been the primary concern of mankind. How is it possible to study something so vulnerable and fleeting? How is it possible to study that which does the studying? How indeed can I study the 'I' that employs the very consciousness needed for the study? These questions will occupy us in a later part of this book. Before we can turn to them directly, we shall do well to take a closer look at the four great Levels of Being: how, with the intervention of additional powers, there are *essential* changes, even though similarities and 'correspondences' remain.

Matter (m), life (x), consciousness (y), self-awareness (z)—

these four elements are ontologically, that is in their fundamental nature, different, incomparable, incommensurable and
discontinuous. Only one of them is directly accessible to
objective, scientific observation by means of our five senses.
The other three are none the less known to us because we ourselves, every one of us, can verify their existence from our own
inner experience.

We never find life except as living matter; we never find
consciousness except as conscious living matter; and we never
find self-awareness except as self-aware, conscious, living
matter. The ontological differences of these four elements are
analogous to the discontinuity of dimensions. A line is one-
dimensional; and no elaboration of a line, no subtlety in its
construction and no complexity, can ever turn it into a surface.
Equally, no elaboration of a two-dimensional surface, no
increase in complexity, subtlety, or size, can ever turn it into a
solid. Existence in the physical world, we know, is attained
only by three-dimensional beings. One- or two-dimensional
things exist only in our minds. Analogically speaking, it might
be said that only man has 'real' existence in this world in so far
as he alone possesses the 'three dimensions' of life, consciousness and self-awareness. In this sense, animals, with only two
dimensions—life and consciousness—have but a shadowy
existence; and plants, lacking the dimensions of self-awareness
and consciousness, relate to a human being as a line relates to a
solid. In terms of this analogy, matter, lacking the three
'invisible dimensions', has no more reality than a geometrical
point.

This analogy, which may seem far-fetched from a logical
point of view, points to an inescapable existential truth: The
most 'real' world we live in is that of our fellow human beings.
Without them, we should experience a sense of enormous
emptiness; we could hardly be human ourselves, for we are
made or marred by our relations with other people. The
company of animals could console us only because, and to the
extent to which, they are reminders, even caricatures, of
human beings. A world without fellow human beings would
be an eerie and unreal place of banishment; with neither
fellow humans nor animals the world would be a dreadful
wasteland, no matter how luscious its vegetation. To call it

one-dimensional would not seem to be an exaggeration. Human existence in a totally inanimate environment, if it were possible, would be total emptiness, total despair. It may seem absurd to pursue such a line of thought; but it is surely not so absurd as a view that counts as 'real' only inanimate matter and treats as 'unreal', 'subjective' and therefore scientifically non-existent the invisible dimensions of life, consciousness and self-awareness.

A simple inspection of the four great Levels of Being has led us to the recognition of the four elements—matter, life, consciousness and self-awareness. It is this recognition that matters, not the precise association of the four elements with the Levels of Being. If the natural scientists should come and tell us that there are some beings that they call animals in whom no trace of consciousness can be detected, it is not for us to argue with them. Recognition is one thing; identification quite another. For us, only recognition is important, and we are entitled to choose typical and fully developed specimens from each Level of Being for our purposes. They manifest and demonstrate most clearly the 'invisible dimensions' of life, consciousness and self-awareness, and this demonstration is not nullified or invalidated by any difficulty of classification in other cases.

Once we have recognised the ontological gaps and discontinuities that separate the four 'elements'—m, x, y, z—from one another, we know also that there can be no 'links' or 'transitional forms'. Life is either present or absent—there cannot be a half-presence—and the same goes for consciousness and self-awareness. Difficulties of identification are often exacerbated by the fact that the lower level tends to produce a kind of mimicry or counterfeit of the higher, just as an animated puppet can at times be mistaken for a living person, or a two-dimensional picture can look like three-dimensional reality. But neither the difficulties of identification and demarcation nor the possibilities of deception and error can be used as arguments against the existence of the four great Levels of Being, exhibiting the four 'elements' that we have called matter, life, consciousness and self-awareness. These four 'elements' are four irreducible mysteries, which need to be most carefully observed and studied, but cannot be explained, let alone 'explained away'.

In a hierarchic structure, the higher does not merely possess powers that are additional to and exceed those possessed by the lower: it also has power *over* the lower, the power of organising the lower and using it for its own purposes. Living beings organise and utilise inanimate matter; conscious beings can utilise life, and self-aware beings can utilise consciousness. Are there powers that are higher than self-awareness? Are there Levels of Being above the human? At this stage in our investigation we need not do more than register the fact that the great majority of mankind, throughout its known history, until very recently, has been unshakenly convinced that the Chain of Being extends upward beyond man. This universal conviction is impressive both for its duration and its intensity. Those individuals of the past whom we still consider the wisest and greatest not only shared this belief but considered it of all truths the most important and the most profound.

3

Progressions

I

The four great Levels of Being exhibit certain characteristics in a manner which I shall call *progressions*. Perhaps the most striking progression is the movement from passivity to activity. At the lowest level, that of 'minerals' or inanimate matter, there is pure passivity. A stone is wholly passive, a pure object, totally dependent on circumstances and 'contingent'. It can do nothing, organise nothing, utilise nothing. Even radioactive material is totally passive. A plant is mainly, but not totally, passive; it is not a pure object; there is a certain, limited ability of adaptation to changing circumstances: it grows towards the light and extends its roots towards moisture and nutrients in the soil. A plant is to a small extent a *subject* with its own power of doing, organising and utilising. It can even be said that there is an intimation of active intelligence in plants — not, of course, as active as that of animals. At the level of 'animal', through the appearance of consciousness there is a striking shift from passivity to activity. The processes of life are speeded up; activity becomes more autonomous, as evidenced by free and often purposeful movement — not merely a gradual turning towards light but a swift action to obtain food or escape danger. The power of doing, organising and utilising is immeasurably extended; there is evidence of an 'inner life', of happiness and unhappiness, confidence, fear, expectation, disappointment and so forth.

Any being with an inner life cannot be a mere object: it is a subject itself, capable even of treating other beings as mere objects, as the cat treats the mouse. At the human level, there is a subject that says 'I' — a person: another marked change

37

from passivity to activity, from object to subject. To treat a person as if he or she were a mere object is a perversity, not to say a crime. No matter how much a person may be weighed down and enslaved by circumstances, there is always the possibility of self-assertion and a rising above circumstances. Man can achieve a measure of control over his environment and thereby his life, utilising things around him for his own purposes. There is no definable limit to his possibilities, even though there are everywhere practical limitations which he has to recognise and respect.

The progressive movement from passivity to activity, which we observe when reviewing the four Levels of Being, is indeed striking, but it is not complete. A large weight of passivity remains even in the most sovereign and autonomous human being; while he is undoubtedly a subject, he remains in many respects an object—dependent, contingent, pushed around by circumstances. Aware of this, mankind has always used its imagination, or its intuitive powers, to complete the process, to extrapolate (as we might say today) the observed curve to its completion. There was thus conceived a Being, wholly active, wholly sovereign and autonomous; a *Person* above all merely human persons, in no way an object, above all circumstances and contingencies, entirely in control of everything: a *personal* God, the 'Unmoved Mover'. The four Levels of Being are thus seen as pointing to the invisible existence of a Level (or Levels) of Being above the human.

An interesting and instructive aspect of the progression from passivity to activity is the change in the origination of movement. It is clear that, at the level of inanimate matter, there cannot be change of movement without a physical cause, and that there is a very close linkage between cause and effect. At the level of plant the causal chain is more complex: physical causes will have physical effects as at the lower level—the wind will shake the tree whether it is living or dead—but certain physical factors act not simply as physical cause but simultaneously as *stimulus*. The sun's rays cause the plant to turn towards the sun. Its leaning too much in one direction causes the roots on the opposite side to grow stronger. At the animal level, again, causation of movement becomes still more complex. An animal can be pushed around like a stone; it can also be stimulated like a plant; but there is in addition a third causative factor which comes from inside: certain drives, attractions or compulsions of a totally non-physical kind; they can be called *motives*. A dog is motivated, and therefore moved, not simply by physical forces or stimuli impinging upon it from the outside, but also by forces originating in its 'inner space': recognising its master, it jumps for joy; recognising its enemy, it runs in fear.

While at the animal level the motivating cause has to be physically present to be effective, at the level of man there is no such need. The power of self-awareness adds for him another possibility of the origination of movement—*will*, that is, the power to move and act even when there is no physical compulsion, no physical stimulus and no motivating force actually present. There is a lot of controversy about will. How free is will? We shall deal with this matter later. In the present context it is merely necessary to recognise that there is at the human level an additional possibility of the origination of movement—one that does not seem to exist at any lower level, namely, movement on the basis of what might be called 'naked insight'. A person might move to another place not because present conditions motivate him to do so, but because he anticipates in his mind certain future developments. While these additional possibilities—the power of foreknowledge and therewith the power of anticipating future possibilities—are no doubt possessed, to some degree, by all human beings, it is evident that they vary greatly and with most of us are very weak. It is possible to imagine a supra-human Level of Being where they would exist in perfection. Perfect foreknowledge of the future would therefore be considered a divine attribute, associated with perfect freedom of movement and perfect freedom from passivity. The progression from physical cause to stimulus to motive and to will would then be completed by a perfection of will capable of overriding all the causative forces that operate at the four Levels of Being known to us.

II

The progression from passivity to activity is similar and closely related to the progression from necessity to freedom. It is easy to see that at the mineral level there is nothing but necessity. Inanimate matter is what it is and cannot be other; there is no choice, no possibility of 'developing' or in any way changing its nature. The so-called indeterminacy at the level of nuclear particles is simply another manifestation of necessity, because total necessity means the absence of any creative principle. As I have said before, it is analogous to the zero dimension — a kind of nothingness which, at the extreme, means that there remains nothing to be determined. The 'freedom' of indeterminacy is in fact the extreme opposite of freedom: a kind of necessity that can be understood only in terms of statistical probability. At the level of inanimate matter, there is no 'inner space' where any autonomous powers could be marshalled. As we shall see, *'inner space' is the scene of freedom.* We know little, if anything, about the 'inner space' of plants, more of that of animals, and a great deal about the 'inner space' of the human being: the space of the person, of creativity, of freedom. Inner space is created by the powers of life, consciousness and self-awareness; but we have direct and personal experience only of our own 'inner space' and the freedom it affords *us*. Close observation discloses that most of us, most of the time, behave and act mechanically, like a machine. The specifically human power of self-awareness is asleep, and the human being, like an animal, acts — more or less intelligently — solely in response to outside influences. Only when a man makes use of his power of self-awareness does he attain to the level of a person, to the level of freedom. At that moment he is living, not being lived. There are still numerous forces of necessity, accumulated in the past, which determine his actions; but a small dent is being made, a tiny change of direction is being introduced. It may be virtually unnoticeable, but many moments of self-awareness can produce many such changes and even turn a given movement into the opposite of its previous direction.

To ask whether the human being has freedom is like asking whether man is a millionaire. He is not, but can become, a millionaire. He can make it his aim to become rich; similarly, he can make it his aim to become free. In his 'inner space' he can develop a centre of strength so that the power of his freedom exceeds that of his necessity. It is possible to imagine a perfect being who is always and invariably exercising his power of self-awareness, which is the power of freedom, to the fullest degree, unmoved by any necessity. This would be a Divine Being, an almighty and sovereign power, a perfect Unity.

III

There is also a marked and unmistakable progression towards integration and unity. At the mineral level, there is no integration. Inanimate matter can be divided and subdivided without loss of character or Gestalt, simply because at this level there is nothing to lose. Even at plant level inner unity is so weak that parts of the plant can often be cut off and will continue to live and develop as separate beings. Animals, by contrast, are much more highly integrated beings. Seen as a biological system, the higher animal is a unity, and parts of it cannot survive separation. There is, however, but little integration on the mental plane; that is to say, even the highest animal attains only a very modest level of logicality and consistency; its memory, on the whole, is weak, and its intellect shadowy.

Man has obviously much more inner unity than any being below him, although integration, as modern psychology recognises, is not guaranteed to him at birth and remains one of his major tasks. As a biological system, he is most harmoniously integrated; on the mental plane, integration is less perfect but is capable of considerable improvement through schooling. As a person, however, a being with the power of self-awareness, he is generally so poorly integrated that he experiences himself as an assembly of many different personalities, each saying 'I'. The classic expression of this experience is found in St Paul's letter to the Romans:

> My own behaviour baffles me. For I find myself not doing what I really want to do but doing what I really loathe. Yet surely if I do things that I really don't want to do, it cannot be said that 'I' am doing them at all—it must be sin that has made its home in my nature. [Rom. VII.14ff, Phillips translation]

Integration means the creation of an inner unity, a centre

of strength and freedom, so that the being ceases to be a mere object, acted upon by outside forces, and becomes a subject, acting from its own 'inner space' into the space outside itself. One of the greatest scholastic statements on this *progression of integration* is found in the *Summa contra Gentiles* by St Thomas Aquinas:

> Of all things the inanimate obtain the lowest place, and from them no emanation is possible except by the action of one on another: thus, fire is engendered from fire when an extraneous body is transformed by fire, and receives the quality and form of fire.
>
> The next place to inanimate bodies belongs to plants, whence emanation proceeds from within, for as much as the plant's intrinsic humour is converted into seed, which being committed to the soil grows into a plant. Accordingly, here we find the first traces of life: since living things are those which move themselves to act, whereas those which can only move extraneous things are wholly lifeless. It is a sign of life in plants that something within them is the cause of a form. Yet the plant's life is imperfect because, although in it emanation proceeds from within, that which emanates comes forth by little and little, and in the end becomes altogether extraneous: thus the humour of a tree gradually comes forth from the tree and eventually becomes a blossom, and then takes the form of fruit, distinct from the branch, though united thereto; and when the fruit is perfect it is altogether severed from the tree, and falling to the ground, produces by its seminal force another plant. Indeed if we consider the matter carefully we shall see that the first principle of this emanation is something extraneous: since the intrinsic humour of the tree is drawn through the roots from the soil whence the plant derives its nourishment.
>
> There is yet above that of the plants a higher form of life, which is that of the sensitive soul, the proper emanation whereof, though beginning from without, terminates within. Also, the further the emanation proceeds, the more does it penetrate within: for the sensible object impresses a form on the external senses, whence it proceeds

to the imagination and, further still, to the storehouse of
the memory. Yet in every process of this kind of emanation, the beginning and the end are in different subjects:
for no sensitive power reflects on itself. Wherefore this
degree of life transcends that of plants in so much as it is
more intimate; and yet it is not a perfect life, since the
emanation is always from one thing to another. Wherefore the highest degree of life is that which is according to
the intellect: for the intellect reflects on itself, and can
understand itself. There are, however, various degrees in
the intellectual life: because the human mind, though able
to know itself, takes its first step to knowledge from without: for it cannot understand apart from phantasms ...
Accordingly, intellectual life is more perfect in the angels
whose intellect does not proceed from something extrinsic
to acquire self-knowledge, but knows itself by itself. Yet
their life does not reach the highest degree of perfection ...
because in them to understand and to be are not the same
thing ... Therefore, the highest perfection of life belongs to
God, whose understanding is not distinct from His
being ... [1]

This statement, unfamiliar as its mode of reasoning may be
to the modern reader, makes it very clear that 'higher' always
means and implies 'more inner', 'more interior', 'deeper',
'more intimate'; while 'lower' means and implies 'more
outer', 'more external'; 'shallower', 'less intimate'. This
synonymity can be found in many languages, perhaps in all of
them.

The more 'interior' a thing is, the less visible it is likely to be.
The *progression* from visibility to invisibility is just another facet
of the great hierarchy of Levels of Being. There is no need to
dwell on it at length. Obviously the terms 'visibility' and
'invisibility' refer not merely to the visual sense but to all
senses of external observation. The powers of life, consciousness and self-awareness that come into focus as we review the
four Levels of Being are all wholly invisible, without colour,
sound, 'skin', taste or smell, and also without extension or
weight. Nevertheless, who would deny that they are what we
are mainly interested in? When I buy a packet of seeds my

main interest is that the contents should be alive and not dead, and an unconscious cat, even though still alive, is not a real cat for me until it has regained consciousness. The invisibility of man has been incisively described by Maurice Nicoll:

> We can all see another person's body directly. We see the lips moving, the eyes opening and shutting, the lines of the mouth and face changing, and the body expressing itself as a whole in action. The person *himself* is invisible ...
>
> If the invisible side of people were discerned as easily as the visible side, we would live in a *new humanity*. As we are, we live in visible humanity, a humanity of *appearances* ...
>
> All our thoughts, emotions, feelings, imaginations, reveries, dreams, fantasies, are *invisible*. All that belongs to our scheming, planning, secrets, ambitions, all our hopes, fears, doubts, perplexities, all our affections, speculations, ponderings, vacuities, uncertainties, all our desires, longings, appetites, sensations, our likes, dislikes, aversions, attractions, loves and hates — all are themselves invisible. They constitute 'oneself'.[2]

Dr Nicoll insists that, while all this may appear obvious, it is not at all obvious: 'It is an extremely difficult thing to grasp ... '

> We do not grasp that we are invisible. We do not realise that we are in a world of invisible people. We do not understand *that life, before all other definitions of it, is a drama of the visible and the invisible.*[3]

There is the external world in which things are visible, i.e. directly accessible to our senses; and there is 'inner space', where things are invisible, i.e. not directly accessible to us, except in the case of ourselves. This all-important point will occupy us at some length in a later chapter.

The progression from the wholly visible mineral to the largely invisible person can be taken as a pointer towards Levels of Being above man which would be totally invisible to our senses, just as there is total visibility at the other end of the scale, the level of minerals. We need not be surprised that most people throughout most of human history implicitly believed in the reality of this projection; they have always claimed that, just as we can learn to 'see' into the invisibility of the persons around us, so we can develop abilities to 'see' the totally invisible beings existing at levels above us.

(As a philosophical map-reader I have the duty to put these important matters on my map, so that it can be seen where they belong and how they connect with other, more familiar, things. Whether or not any reader, traveller or pilgrim wishes to explore them is his own affair.)

IV

The degree of integration, of inner coherence and strength, is closely related to the kind of 'world' that exists for beings at different levels. Inanimate matter has no 'world'. Its total passivity is equivalent to the total emptiness of its world. A plant has a 'world' of its own—a bit of soil, water, air, light and possibly other influences a 'world' limited to its modest biological needs. The world of any one of the higher animals is incomparably greater and richer, although still mainly determined by biological needs, as modern animal psychology studies have amply demonstrated. But there is also something more—like curiosity—which enlarges the animal's world beyond the narrow biological confines.

The world of man, again, is incomparably greater and richer; indeed, it is asserted in traditional philosophy that man is *capax universi*, capable of bringing the whole universe into his experience. What he will actually grasp depends on each person's own Level of Being. The 'higher' the person, the greater and richer is his or her world. A person, for instance, entirely fixed in the philosophy of materialistic scientism, denying the reality of the 'invisibles' and confining his attention solely to what can be counted, measured and weighed, lives in a very poor world, so poor that he will experience it as a meaningless wasteland unfit for human habitation. Equally, if he sees it as nothing but an accidental collocation of atoms he will needs agree with Bertrand Russell that the only rational attitude is one of 'unyielding despair'.

It has been said (by Gurdjieff to his pupils), 'Your Level of Being attracts your life.' There are no occult or unscientific assumptions behind this saying. At a low Level of Being only a very poor world exists and only a very impoverished kind of life can be lived. The Universe is what it is; but he who, although *capax universi*, limits himself to its lowest sides — to his biological needs, his creature comforts or his accidental encounters — will inevitably 'attract' a miserable life. If he can recognise nothing but 'struggle for survival' and 'will to power' fortified by cunning, his 'world' will be one fitting Hobbes's description of the life of man as 'solitary, poor, nasty, brutish, and short'.

The higher the Level of Being, the greater, richer and more wonderful is the world. If we again extrapolate beyond the human level, we can understand why the Divine was considered not merely *capax universi* but actually in total possession of it, aware of everything, omniscient — 'Are not five sparrows sold for two farthings, and not one of them is forgotten before God' (Luke XII.6).

If we take the 'fourth dimension' — time — into consideration a similar picture emerges. At the lowest level, there is time only in the sense of duration. For creatures endowed with consciousness there is time in the sense of experience; but experience is confined to the present, except where the past is made present through memory (of one kind or another), and the future is made present through foresight (of which, again, there may be different kinds). The higher the Level of Being, the 'broader', as it were, is the present; the more it embraces of what, at lower Levels of Being, is past and future. At the highest imaginable Level of Being there would be the *'eternal now'*. Something like this may be the meaning of this passage in Rev. X.5,6:

> And the angel which I saw stand upon the sea and upon the earth lifted up his hand to heaven, and sware by him that liveth for ever and ever, who created heaven, and the things that therein are, and the earth, and the things that therein are, and the sea, and the things which are therein, that there should be time no longer.

V

An almost infinite number of further 'progressions' could be added to those already described; but this is not the purpose of this book. The reader will be able to fill in whatever seems to him to be of special interest. Maybe he is interested in the question of 'final causes'. Is it legitimate to explain or even to describe a given phenomenon in teleological terms, i.e. as pursuing a purpose? It is ridiculous to answer such a question without reference to the Level of Being at which the pheno- menon is situated. To deny teleological action at the human level would be as foolish as to impute it at the level of inanimate matter. Hence there is no reason to assume that traces or remnants of teleological action could not be found at the levels in between.

The four great Levels of Being can be likened to an inverted pyramid where each higher level comprises everything lower and is open to influences from everything higher. All the four levels exist in the human being, which, as we have already seen, can be described by the formula

Man $= m + x + y + z$

$= $ mineral $+$ life $+$ consciousness $+$ self-awareness.

Not surprisingly, many teachings describe man as possessing four 'bodies', namely,

the physical body (corresponding to m);
the etheric body (corresponding to x);
the astral body (corresponding to y); and
the 'I' or Ego or
  Self or Spirit (corresponding to z).

In the light of our understanding of the four great Levels of Being, such descriptions of man as a fourfold being become easily comprehensible. In some teachings, $m + x$, is taken as one—the living body (because an inanimate body is of no interest at all), and they therefore speak of man as a threefold being, consisting of body $(m + x)$, soul (y) and Spirit (z). As people turned their interests increasingly to the visible world the distinction between soul and Spirit became more difficult to maintain and tended to be dropped altogether; man, therefore, was represented as a being compounded of body and soul. With the rise of materialistic scientism, finally, even the souls disappeared from the description of man—how could it exist when it could be neither weighed nor measured?—except as one of the many strange attributes of complex arrangements of atoms and molecules. Why not accept the so-called 'soul'—

a bundle of surprising powers—as an *epiphenomenon* of matter just as, say, magnetism has been accepted as such? The Universe was no longer seen as a great hierarchical structure or Chain of Being; it was seen simply as an accidental collocation of atoms; and man, traditionally understood as the microcosm reflecting the macrocosm (i.e. the structure of the Universe), was no longer seen as a *cosmos*, a meaningful even though mysterious creation. If the great Cosmos is seen as nothing but a chaos of particles without purpose or meaning, so man must be seen as nothing but a chaos of particles without purpose and meaning—a sensitive chaos, indeed, capable of suffering pain, anguish and despair, but a chaos all the same (whether he likes it or not)—a rather unfortunate cosmic accident of no consequence whatsoever.

This is the picture presented by modern materialistic scientism, and the only question is, does it make sense of what we can actually experience? This is a question everybody has to decide for himself. Those who stand in awe and admiration, in wonder and also in perplexity, contemplating the four great Levels of Being, will not be easily persuaded that there is only more or less—i.e. horizontal extension. They will find it impossible to close their minds to 'higher' or 'lower'—that is to say, to vertical scales and even discontinuities. If they then see man as *higher* than any arrangement, no matter how complex, of inanimate matter, and *higher* than the animals, no matter how far advanced, they will also see man as 'open-ended', not at the highest level but with a potential that might indeed lead up to perfection. This is the most important insight that follows from the contemplation of the four great Levels of Being: at the level of man, there is no discernible limit or ceiling. Self-awareness, which constitutes the difference between animal and man, is a power of unlimited potential, a power that not only makes man human, but gives him the possibility, even the need, to become superhuman. As the scholastics used to say, 'Homo non proprie humanus sed superhumanus est', which means that, to be properly human, you must go beyond the merely human.

4

Adaequatio I

What enables man to know anything at all about the world around him? 'Knowing demands the organ fitted to the object', said Plotinus (d. A.D. 270). Nothing can be known without there being an appropriate 'instrument' in the makeup of the knower. This is the Great Truth of *adaequatio* (adequateness), which defines knowledge as *adaequatio rei et intellectus*: the understanding of the knower must be *adequate* to the thing to be known.

From Plotinus, again, comes the famous saying: 'Never did eye see the sun unless it had first become sunlike, and never can the soul have vision of the First Beauty unless itself be beautiful.' John Smith the Platonist (1618–52) said: 'That which enables us to know and understand aright in the things of God, must be a living principle of holiness within us'; to which we might add the statement by St Thomas Aquinas (1225–74) that 'knowledge comes about in so far as the object known is within the knower.'

We have seen already that man, in a sense, *comprises* the four great Levels of Being; there is therefore some degree of correspondence or 'connaturality' between the structure of man and the structure of the world. This is a very ancient idea and has usually been expressed by calling man a 'microcosm' which somehow 'corresponds' with the 'macrocosm' which is the world. He is a physico-chemical system, like the rest of the world, and he also possesses the invisible and mysterious powers of life, consciousness and self-awareness, some or all of which he can detect in many beings around him.

Our five bodily senses make us 'adequate' to the lowest

49

Level of Being—inanimate matter. But they can supply nothing more than masses of sense-data, to 'make sense' of which we require abilities or capabilities of a different order. We may call them 'intellectual senses'. Without them, we should be unable to recognise form, pattern, regularity, harmony, rhythm and meaning, not to mention life, consciousness and self-awareness. While the bodily senses may be described as relatively passive, mere receivers of what happens to come along and to a large extent controlled by the mind, the intellectual senses are the *mind-in-action*, and their keenness and reach are qualities of the mind itself. As regards the bodily senses, all healthy people possess a very similar endowment; but no one could possibly overlook the fact that there are significant differences in the power and reach of people's minds. As regards the intellectual senses, it is therefore quite unrealistic to try to define and delimit the capabilities of 'man' as such—as if all human beings were much the same, like animals of the same species. Beethoven's musical abilities, even in deafness, were incomparably greater than mine, and the difference did not lie in the sense of hearing; it lay in the mind. Some people are incapable of grasping and appreciating a given piece of music, not because they are deaf, but because of a lack of *adaequatio* in the mind. The sense of hearing receives nothing more than a succession of notes; the music is grasped by intellectual powers. Some people possess these powers to such a degree that they can grasp, and also retain in their memory, an entire symphony on the strength of one hearing or one reading of the score; while others are so weakly endowed that they cannot absorb it at all, no matter how often and how attentively they listen to it. For the former the symphony is as real as it was to the composer; for the latter, there is no symphony: there is nothing but a succession of more or less agreeable but altogether meaningless noises. The former's mind is *adequate* to the symphony; the latter's mind is *inadequate*, and thus incapable of recognising the existence of the symphony. The same applies throughout the whole range of possible and actual human experiences. For every one of us, only those facts and phenomena 'exist' for which we possess *adaequatio*, and as we are not entitled to assume that we are necessarily adequate to everything, at all times, and in whatever condition we may find ourselves, so we are not entitled to insist that something inaccessible to us has no existence at all and is nothing but a phantom of other people's imagination.

There are physical facts which the bodily senses pick up; but there are also non-physical facts which remain unnoticed unless the work of the senses is controlled and completed by certain 'higher' faculties of the mind. Some of these non-physical facts represent 'grades of significance', to use a term coined by the late Mr G. N. M. Tyrrell, who gives the following illustration:

> Take a book, for example. To an animal a book is merely a coloured shape. Any higher significance a book may hold lies above the level of its thought. And the book *is* a coloured shape; the animal is not wrong. To go a step higher, an uneducated savage may regard a book as a series of marks on paper. This is the book as seen on a higher level of significance than the animal's, and one which corresponds to the savage's level of thought. Again it is not wrong, only the book *can* mean more. It may mean a series of letters arranged according to certain rules. This is the book on a higher level of significance than the savage's ... Or finally, on a still higher level, the book may be an expression of meaning ... [1]

In all these cases the 'sense data' are the same; the facts given to the eye are identical. Not the eye, only the mind, can determine the 'grade of significance'. People say: 'Let the facts speak for themselves'; they forget that the speech of facts is real only if it is heard and understood. It is thought to be an easy matter to distinguish between fact and theory, between perception and interpretation. In truth, it is extremely difficult. You see the full moon just above the horizon against the silhouettes of some trees or buildings — and it appears to you as a disc as large as that of the sun; but the full moon straight above your head looks quite small. What are the moon images actually received by the eye? They are exactly the same in both cases. And yet, even when you know this to be so, your mind will not easily let you see the two discs as of equal size. 'Perception is not determined simply by the stimulus pattern', writes R. L. Gregory in *Eye and Brain*; 'rather it is a dynamic searching for the best interpretation of the available data.'[2] This searching uses not only the sensory information but also other knowledge and experience, although just how far experience affects perception, according to Gregory, is a difficult question to answer. In short, we 'see' not simply with our eyes but with a great part of our mental equipment as well, and since this mental equipment varies greatly from person to person, there are inevitably many things which some people can 'see' while others cannot, or, to put it differently, for which some people are *adequate* while others are not.

When the level of the knower is not adequate to the level (or grade of significance) of the object of knowledge, the result is not factual error but something much more serious: an inadequate and impoverished view of reality. Mr Tyrrell pursues his illustration further, as follows:

> A book, we will suppose, has fallen into the hands of intelligent beings who know nothing of what writing and printing mean, but they are accustomed to dealing with the external relationships of things. They try to find out the 'laws' of the book, which for them mean the principles governing the order in which the letters are arranged ... They will think they have discovered the laws of the book when they have formulated certain rules governing the external relationships of the letters. That each word and each sentence expresses a meaning will never dawn on them because their background of thought is made up of concepts which deal only with external relationships, and explanation to them means solving the puzzle of these external relationships ... Their methods will never reach the grade [of significance] which contains the idea of meanings.[3]

Just as the world is an hierarchical structure, with regard to which it is meaningful to speak of 'higher' and 'lower', so the senses, organs, powers and other 'instruments' by which the human being perceives and gains knowledge of the world form an hierarchical structure of 'higher' and 'lower'. 'As above, so below', the Ancients used to say: to the world outside us there corresponds, in some fashion, a world inside us. And just as the higher levels in the world are rarer, more exceptional, than the lower levels—mineral matter is ubiquitous; life only a thin film on the Earth; consciousness, relatively rare; and self-awareness, the great exception—so it is with the abilities of people. The lowest abilities, such as seeing and also counting, belong to every normal person, while the higher abilities, such as those needed for the perceiving and grasping of the more subtle aspects of reality, are less and less widely available as we move up the scale.

There are inequalities in the human endowment, but they are probably of much less importance than are differences in interests and in what Mr Tyrrell calls the 'background of thought'. The intelligent beings of Mr Tyrrell's allegory lacked *adaequatio* with regard to the book because they based themselves on the assumption that the 'external relationships of the letters' were all that mattered. They were what we should call scientific materialists whose faith is that objective reality is limited to that which can be actually observed and who are ruled by a methodical aversion against the recognition of higher levels or grades of significance.

The level of significance to which an observer or investigator tries to attune himself is chosen, not by his intelligence, but by his faith. The facts themselves, which he is going to observe, do not carry a label indicating the appropriate level at which they ought to be considered. Nor does the choice of an inadequate level lead the intelligence into factual error or logical contradiction. All levels of significance *up to* the adequate level— i.e. up to the level of meaning, in the example of the book—are equally factual, equally logical, equally objective, but not equally *real*.

It is by an act of faith that I choose the level of my investigation; hence the saying 'Credo ut intelligam'—I have faith so as to be able to understand. If I lack faith, and consequently choose an inadequate level of significance for my investigation, no degree of 'objectivity' will ever save me from missing the point of the whole thing, and I rob myself of the very possibility of understanding. I shall then be one of those of whom it has been said: 'They, seeing, see not; and hearing they hear not, neither do they understand.'[4]

In short, when dealing with something representing a higher grade of significance or Level of Being than inanimate matter, the observer depends not only on the adequateness of his own higher qualities, perhaps 'developed' through learning and training; he also depends on the adequateness of his 'faith' or, to put it more conventionally, of his fundamental presuppositions and basic assumptions. In this respect he tends to be very much a child of his time and of the civilisation in which he has spent his formative years; for the human mind, generally speaking, does not just think: it thinks with ideas, most of which it simply adopts and takes over from surrounding society.

There is nothing more difficult than to become critically aware of the presuppositions of one's thought. Everything can be seen directly except the eye through which we see. Every thought can be scrutinised directly except the thought by which we scrutinise. A special effort, an effort of self-awareness, is needed—that almost impossible feat of thought recoiling upon itself: almost impossible but not quite. In fact, this is the power that makes man human and also capable of transcending his humanity. It lies in what the Bible calls man's 'inward parts'. As mentioned already, inward corresponds with 'higher' and outward corresponds with 'lower'. The senses are man's most outward instruments; when there is a case of 'they, seeing, see not, and hearing, they hear not' the fault does not lie with the senses but with the inward parts—'for this people's heart is waxed gross'; they fail to 'understand with their heart'.[5] Only through the 'heart' can contact be made with the higher grades of significance and Levels of Being.

For anyone wedded to the materialistic scientism of the modern age it will be impossible to understand what this means. He has no belief in anything higher than man, and he sees in man nothing but a relatively highly evolved animal. He insists that truth can be discovered only by means of the brain, which is situated in the head and not in the heart. All this means that 'understanding with one's heart' is to him a meaningless collection of words. From his point of view, he is quite right: the brain, situated in the head and supplied with data by the bodily senses, is fully adequate for dealing with inanimate matter, the lowest of the four great Levels of Being. Indeed, its working would only be disturbed and possibly be distorted if the 'heart' interfered in any way. As a materialistic scientist, he believes that life, consciousness and self-awareness are nothing but manifestations of complex arrangements of inanimate particles— a 'faith' which makes it perfectly rational for him to place exclusive reliance on the bodily senses, to 'stay in the head', and to reject any interference from the 'powers' situated in the heart. For him, in other words, higher levels of reality simply do not exist, *because his faith excludes the possibility of their existence.* He is like a man who, although in possession of a radio receiver, refuses to use it because he has made up his mind that nothing but atmospheric noises can be obtained from it.

Faith is not in conflict with reason; nor is it a substitute for reason. Faith chooses the grade of significance or Level of Being at which the search for knowledge and understanding is to aim. There is reasonable faith and also unreasonable faith. To look for meaning and purpose at the level of inanimate matter would be as unreasonable an act of faith as an attempt to 'explain' the masterpieces of human genius as nothing but the outcome of economic interests or sexual frustrations. The faith of the agnostic is perhaps the most unreasonable of all, because, unless it is mere camouflage, it is a decision to treat the question of significance as insignificant, like saying: 'I am not willing to decide whether [reverting to Mr Tyrrell's example] a book is merely a coloured shape, a series of marks on paper, a series of letters arranged according to certain rules or an expression of meaning.' Not surprisingly, traditional wisdom has always treated the agnostic with withering contempt: 'I know thy works, that thou are neither cold nor hot: I would thou wert cold or hot. So then because thou art lukewarm, and neither cold nor hot, I will spue thee out of my mouth.'[6]

It can hardly be taken as an unreasonable act of faith when people accept the testimony of prophets, sages and saints who, in different languages but with virtually one voice, declare that the book of this world is not merely a coloured shape but an expression of meaning; that there are Levels of Being above that of humanity; and that man can reach these higher levels provided he allows his reason to be guided by faith. No one has described man's possible journey to the truth more clearly than the Bishop of Hippo, St Augustine (A.D. 354–430):

The first step forward ... will be to see that the attention is fastened on truth. Of course faith does not see truth clearly, but it has an eye for it, so to speak, which enables it to see that a thing is true even when it does not see the reason for it. It does not yet see the thing it believes, but at least it knows for certain that it does not see it and that it is true none the less. This possession through faith of a hidden but certain truth is the very thing which will impel the mind to penetrate its content, and to give the formula, 'Believe that you may understand' (*Crede ut intelligas*), its full meaning.[7]

We can see things with the light of the intellect which are invisible to our bodily senses. No one denies that mathematical and geometrical truths are 'seen' in this way. To *prove* a proposition means to give it a form, by analysis, simplification, transformation, or dissection, through which the truth can be seen: beyond this seeing there is neither the possibility of, nor the need for, any further proof.

Can we see, with the light of the intellect, things that go beyond mathematics and geometry? Again, no one denies that we can *see* what another person means, sometimes even when he does not express himself accurately. Our everyday language is a constant witness to this power of seeing, of grasping ideas, which is quite different from the processes of thinking and forming opinions. It produces flashes of understanding.

As far as St Augustine is concerned, faith is the heart of the matter. *Faith tells us what there is to understand*; it purifies the heart, and so allows reason to profit from discussion; it enables reason to arrive at an understanding of God's revelation. In short, when Augustine speaks of understanding, he always has in mind the product of a rational activity for which faith prepares the way.[8]

Faith opens 'the eye of truth', as the Buddhists say, also called 'the Eye of the Heart' or 'the Eye of the Soul'. St Augustine insisted that 'our whole business in this life is to restore to health the eye of the heart whereby God may be seen.' Persia's greatest Sufi poet, Rumi (1207–73), speaks of 'the eye of the heart, which is seventy-fold and of which these two sensible eyes are only the gleaners';[9] while John Smith the Platonist advises: 'We must shut the eyes of sense, and open that brighter eye of our understandings, that other eye of the soul, as the philosopher calls our intellectual faculty, "which indeed all have, but few make use of it".'[10] The Scottish theologian, Richard of Saint-Victor (d. 1173), says: 'For the outer sense alone perceives visible things and the eye of the heart alone sees the invisible.'[11]

The power of the 'eye of the heart', which produces insight, is vastly superior to the power of thought, which produces *opinions*. 'Recognising the poverty of philosophical opinions,' says the Buddha, 'not adhering to any of them, seeking the truth, *I saw*.'[12] The process of mobilising the various powers possessed by man, gradually and, as it were, organically, is described in a Buddhist text as follows:

> One can not, I say, attain supreme knowledge all at once; only by a gradual training, a gradual action, a gradual unfolding, does one attain perfect knowledge. In what manner? A man comes, moved by confidence; having come, he joins; having joined, he listens; listening, he receives the doctrine; having received the doctrine, he remembers it; he examines the sense of the things remembered; from examining the sense, the things are approved of; having approved, desire is born; he ponders; pondering, he eagerly trains himself; and eagerly training himself, he mentally realises the highest truth itself and, penetrating it by means of wisdom, *he sees*.[13]

This is the process of gaining *adaequatio*, of developing the instrument capable of seeing and thus understanding the truth that does not merely inform the mind but liberates the soul. ('And ye shall know the truth, and the truth shall make you free'—John VIII.32.)

As these matters have become unfamiliar in the modern world, it may be of value if I quote a contemporary author, the late Dr Maurice Nicoll:

> A world of *inward* perception then begins to open out, distinct from that of outer perception. Inner space appears. *The creation of the world begins in man himself*. At first all is

darkness: then light appears and is separated from the darkness. By this light we understand a form of consciousness to which our ordinary consciousness is, by comparison, darkness. This light has constantly been equated with truth and freedom. Inner perception of oneself, of one's invisibility, is the beginning of light. This perception of truth is not a matter of sense-perception, but of the perception of the truth of 'ideas' — through which, certainly, the perception of our senses is greatly increased. The path of self-knowledge has this aim in view, for no one can know himself unless he turns inwards ... This struggle marks the commencement of that inner development of man which has been written about in many different ways (yet really always in the same way) throughout that small part of Time whose literature belongs to us, and which we think of as the entire history of the world.[14]

We shall take a closer look at the process of 'turning inward' in a later chapter. For our present purposes it is necessary simply to recognise that sense data alone do not produce insight or understanding of any kind. *Ideas* produce insight and understanding, and the world of ideas lies within us. The truth of ideas cannot be seen by the senses but only by that special instrument sometimes referred to as 'the eye of the heart' which, in a mysterious way, has the power of recognising truth when confronted with it. If we describe the results of this power as illumination, and the results of the senses as experience, we can say that

experience, and not illumination, tells us about the existence, appearance, and changes of sensible things, such as stones, plants, animals, and people; while illumination, and not experience, tells us what such things mean, what they could be, and what they perhaps ought to be.

Our bodily senses, yielding experience, do not put us into touch with the higher grades of significance and the higher Levels of Being existing in the world around us: they are not adequate for such a purpose, having been designed solely for registering the outer differences between various existing things, and not their inner meanings.

There is a story of two monks who were passionate smokers and tried to settle among themselves the question of whether it was permissible to smoke while praying. As they could not come to a conclusion they decided to ask their respective superiors. One of them got into deep trouble with his abbot; the other received a pat of encouragement. When they met again, the first one, slightly suspicious, inquired of the second: 'What did you actually ask?' and received the answer: 'I asked whether it was permissible to pray while smoking.' While our *inner* senses infallibly see the profound difference between 'praying while smoking' and 'smoking while praying', to our *outer* senses there is no difference at all.

Higher grades of significance and Levels of Being cannot be recognised without faith and the help of the higher abilities of the inner man. When these higher abilities are not brought into action—either because they are lacking or because an absence of faith leaves them unutilised—there is a lack of *adaequatio* on the part of the knower, which produces the effect that nothing of any higher significance or Level of Being can be known by him.

5

Adaequatio II

I

The Great Truth of *adaequatio* affirms that nothing can be perceived without an appropriate organ of perception and nothing can be understood without an appropriate organ of understanding. For cognition at the mineral level, man's primary instruments, as mentioned before, are his five senses, reinforced and extended by a great array of ingenious apparatus. They register the visible world, but cannot register the 'inwardness' of things and such fundamental invisible powers as life, consciousness and self-awareness. Who could see, hear, touch, taste or smell life as such? It has no shape or colour, no specific sound, or texture, or taste, or smell. And yet, as we are able to recognise 'life', we must have an organ of perception to do so, an organ more inward, and that means 'higher', than the senses. We shall see later that this organ is identical with the life inside ourselves, the unconscious vegetative processes and feelings of our living body, centred mainly in the solar plexus. Similarly, we recognise 'consciousness' directly with our own consciousness, centred mainly in the head; and we recognise 'self-awareness' with our own self-awareness, which resides, in a sense that is both symbolical and also verifiable by physical experience, in the heart region, the innermost and therefore 'highest' centre of the human being. (Many people are so little aware of their power of self-awareness that they are incapable of recognising this power in other human beings and therefore take them as nothing but 'higher animals'.)

The answer to the question, 'What are man's instruments by which to know the world outside him?' is therefore quite inescapably this: 'Everything he has got—his living body, his mind and his self-aware Spirit.'

Since Descartes, we are inclined to believe that we know even of our existence only through our head-centred thinking— 'cogito ergo sum'—I think and thus I know I exist. But every craftsman knows that his power of knowing consists not only of the thinking in his head, but also of the intelligence of his body: his fingertips know things that his thinking knows nothing about, just as Pascal (1623–62) knew that 'the heart has its reasons which reason knows nothing about.' It may even be misleading to say that man has many instruments of cognition, since, in fact, the whole man is *one* instrument. If he persuades himself that the only 'data' worth having are those delivered by his five senses, and that a 'data processing unit' called the brain is there to deal with them, he restricts his knowing to that Level of Being for which these instruments are *adequate*, and this means mainly to the level of inanimate matter.

It was Sir Arthur Eddington who said: 'Ideally, all our knowledge of the universe could have been reached by visual sensation alone—in fact by the simplest form of visual sensation, colourless and non-stereoscopic.'[1] If this is true (as it well may be), if the scientific picture of the universe is the result of the use only of the sense of sight, restricted to the use of 'a single, colour-blind eye', we can hardly expect that picture to show more than an abstract, meaningless, inhospitable mechanism. The Great Truth of *adaequatio* teaches us that restriction in the use of instruments of cognition has the inevitable effect of narrowing and impoverishing reality. And this raises a most important question. Surely, nobody *wishes* to obtain this effect; how then can it be explained that such a narrowing has taken place?

To answer this question, we have to turn again to the father of the modern development, Descartes. He was not a man lacking self-confidence. 'The true principles', he said, 'by which we can attain the highest degree of wisdom, which constitutes the sovereign good of human life, are those I have put in this book ... Man has ... had many opinions so far; he has never had "the certain knowledge of anything" ... But now he reaches manhood, he becomes master of himself and capable of adjusting everything to the level of reason.' So Descartes claims to lay the foundations of 'the admirable science', which is built from *'ideas easiest to grasp, the simplest, and which can be most directly represented'*.[2] And what, in the end, is the easiest to grasp, the simplest, and can be most directly represented? Precisely the 'pointer readings' against a quantitative scale, highlighted by Sir Arthur Eddington.[3]

The sense of sight, restricted to the use of a single colour-blind eye, being the lowest, most outward and most superficial (i.e. surface-bound) of man's instruments of cognition, is equally available to every normal person, and so is the ability to count. Needless to say, to *understand* the significance of such data requires some of the higher, and therefore rarer, faculties of the mind; but this is not the point. The point is that once a theory has been advanced—perhaps by a man of genius—anyone who takes the necessary trouble can 'verify' it. Knowledge obtainable from 'pointer readings' is therefore 'public knowledge', available to anyone; precise; indubitable; easy to check; easy to communicate; above all, *virtually untainted by any subjectivity of the observer.*

I said earlier that it is often extremely difficult to get at bare facts unmingled with any thoughts, adjustments or adaptations coming from the observer's mind. But what can the mind add to pointer readings made by a single colour-blind eye? What can it add to counting? Restricting ourselves to this mode of observation, we can indeed eliminate subjectivity and attain objectivity. Yet one restriction entails another. We attain objectivity, but we fail to attain knowledge of the object as a whole: only the 'lowest', the most superficial, aspects of the object are accessible to the instruments we employ—everything that makes the object humanly interesting, meaningful, significant, escapes us. Not surprisingly, the world picture resulting from this methodology of observation is 'the abomination of desolation', a wasteland in which man is a quaint cosmic accident signifying nothing.

Descartes wrote:

It is the mathematicians alone who have been able to find demonstrations ... I did not doubt that I must start with the same things that they have considered ... The long

chains of perfectly simple and easy reasons which geo-
meters are accustomed to employ in order to arrive at their
most difficult demonstrations, had given me reason to
believe that all things which fall under the knowledge of
man succeed each other in the same way and that ... there
can be none so remote that they may not be reached, or so
hidden that they may not be discovered.[4]

It is obvious that a mathematical model of the world—
which is what Descartes was dreaming about—can deal only
with factors that can be expressed as interrelated quantities. It
is equally obvious that (while *pure quantity* is not possible in
manifestation) the quantitative factor is of preponderant
weight only at the lowest Level of Being. As we move up the
Chain of Being, the importance of quantity recedes while that
of quality gains, and the price of mathematical model-building
is the loss of the qualitative factor, the very thing that matters
most.

The change of Western man's interest from 'the slenderest
knowledge that may be obtained of the highest things' (Thomas
Aquinas) to mathematically precise knowledge of the lesser
things—'there being nothing in the world the knowledge of
which would be more desirable or more useful' (Christian
Huygens, 1629–95)—marks a change from what we may call
'science for understanding' to 'science for manipulation'. The
purpose of the former was the enlightenment of the person and
his 'liberation'; the purpose of the latter is power: 'Knowledge
itself is power', said Francis Bacon (1561–1626), and Descartes
promised men to become 'masters and possessors of nature'. In
its further development, 'science for manipulation' almost
inevitably tends to advance from the manipulation of nature to
that of people.

'Science for understanding' has often been called 'wisdom',
while the name of 'science' remained reserved for what I call
'science for manipulation'. St Augustine, among many others,
makes this distinction, and Etienne Gilson paraphrases him as
follows:

The real difference which sets the one against the other
derives from the nature of their objects. The object of
wisdom is such that, by reason of its intelligibility alone, no

evil use can be made of it; the object of science is such that
it is in constant danger of falling into the clutches of
cupidity, owing to its very materiality. Hence the double
designation we may give science according as it is subservient to appetite, as it is whenever it chooses itself as its
end, or is subservient to wisdom, as it is whenever it is
directed towards the sovereign good.[5]

These points are of crucial importance. When 'science for
manipulation' is subordinated to wisdom, i.e. 'science for
understanding', it is a most valuable tool, and no harm can
come of it. But it cannot be so subordinated when wisdom
disappears because people cease to be interested in its pursuit.
This has been the history of Western thought since Descartes.
The old science—'Wisdom', or 'science for understanding'—
was primarily directed 'towards the sovereign good', i.e. the
True, the Good and the Beautiful, the knowledge of which would
bring both happiness and salvation. The new science was
directed mainly towards material power, a tendency that has
meanwhile developed to such lengths that the enhancement of
political and economic power is now generally taken as the
first purpose of, and main justification for, expenditure on
scientific work. The old science looked upon nature as God's
handiwork and man's mother; the new science tends to look
upon it as an adversary to be conquered or a quarry to be
exploited.

The greatest and most influential difference, however,
relates to the attitude of science to man. The 'science for
understanding' saw man as made in the image of God, the
crowning glory of creation, and hence 'in charge' of the world,
because *noblesse oblige*. The 'science for manipulation', inevitably, sees man as nothing but an accidental product of
evolution, a higher animal, a social animal, and an object for
study by the same methods by which other phenomena of this
world were to be studied—'objectively'. Wisdom is a type of
knowledge that can be used only by bringing into play the
highest and noblest powers of the mind; 'science for manipulation', by contrast, is a type of knowledge that can be used by
bringing into play only such powers as are possessed by everybody except the severely handicapped, mainly pointer reading

and counting, without any need to understand why a formula works: to know that it *does* work is enough for practical and manipulative purposes. This type of knowledge is therefore public, i.e. it is describable in terms of general validity, so that, when correctly described, everybody can recognise it. The public and 'democratic' availability of this type of knowledge cannot be attained by knowledge relating to the higher Levels of Being, simply because the latter is not describable in terms to which everybody is *adequate*. It is claimed that only such knowledge can be termed 'scientific' and 'objective' as is open to public verification or falsification by anybody who takes the necessary trouble; all the rest is dismissed as 'unscientific' and 'subjective'. The use of these terms in this manner is a grave abuse, for all knowledge is 'subjective' inasmuch as it cannot exist otherwise than in the mind of a human subject, and the distinction between 'scientific' and 'unscientific' knowledge is question-begging, the only valid question about knowledge being that of its truth.

The progressive elimination of 'science for understanding' — or 'wisdom' — in Western civilisation turns the rapid and ever accelerating accumulation of 'knowledge for manipulation' into a most serious threat. As I have said in another context, 'we are now far too clever to be able to survive without wisdom', and further developments of our cleverness can be of no benefit whatever. The steadily advancing concentration of man's scientific interest on 'sciences of manipulation' has at least three very serious consequences. First, in the absence of sustained study of such 'unscientific' questions as 'What is the meaning and purpose of man's existence?' 'What is good and what is evil?' and 'What are man's absolute rights and duties?', a civilisation will necessarily and inescapably sink ever more deeply into anguish, despair and lack of freedom. People within it will progressively lose health and happiness, no matter how high may be their standard of living or how successful may be their 'health service' in prolonging their lives. It is nothing more or less than a matter of 'man cannot live by bread alone'. Second, the methodical restriction of scientific efforts to the most external and material aspects of the Universe makes the world look so empty and meaningless that even those people who see the value and necessity of a 'science of understanding' cannot escape the hypnotic power of the allegedly scientific picture presented to them, and lose the courage as well as the inclination to consult the 'wisdom tradition of mankind' and to profit from it. Since the findings of science, on account of its methodical restriction and its systematic disregard of higher levels, never contain any evidence of the existence of such higher levels, the process is self-reinforcing: faith, instead of being taken as a guide leading the intellect to an understanding of the higher levels, is seen as opposing and rejecting the intellect and therefore is itself rejected. Thus all roads to recovery are barred. Third, the higher powers of man, no longer being brought into play to produce the knowledge of wisdom, atrophy and even disappear altogether. As a result, all problems that society or individuals are called upon to tackle become insoluble. Efforts become ever more frantic, while unsolved and seemingly insoluble problems accumulate. While wealth may still be accumulating, the quality of man declines.

<h1 style="text-align:center">II</h1>

In the ideal case, the structure of a man's knowledge would match the structure of reality. At the highest level, there would be 'knowledge for understanding' in its purest form; at the lowest, there would be 'knowledge for manipulation'. Understanding is required to decide what to do; the help of 'knowledge for manipulation' is needed to act effectively in the material world.

For successful action, we need to know what will be the results of alternative courses of action, so as to be able to select the course most suitable for our purposes. At this level, therefore, it is correct to say that the goal of knowledge is prediction and control. The pursuit of science is a matter of taking stock and formulating recipes for action. Every recipe is a conditional sentence of the type, 'If you want to achieve this or that, take such and such steps.' The sentence should be as concise as possible, without any ideas or concepts that are not strictly necessary ('Occam's razor'), and the instructions should be precise, leaving as little as possible to the judgment of the operator. The test of a recipe is purely pragmatic—the proof of the pudding being in the eating. The perfections of this type of science are purely practical—objective, i.e. independent of the character and interests of the operator, measurable, recordable, repeatable. Such knowledge is 'public' in the sense that it can be used even by evil men for nefarious purposes; it gives power to anyone who manages to get hold of it. (Not surprisingly, therefore, many attempts are always being made to keep parts of this 'public' knowledge secret!)

At the higher levels, the very ideas of prediction and control become increasingly objectionable and even absurd. The theologian who strives to obtain knowledge of Levels of Being above the human does not for a moment think of prediction, control or manipulation. All he seeks is understanding. He would be shocked by predictabilities. Anything predictable can be so only on account of its 'fixed nature', and the higher the Level of Being, the less is the fixity and the greater the plasticity of nature. 'With God all things are possible' (Matt. XIX.26), but the freedom of action of a hydrogen atom is exceedingly limited. The sciences of inanimate matter—physics, chemistry and astronomy—can therefore achieve virtually perfect powers of prediction; they can in fact be completed and finalised, once and for all, as is claimed to be the case with mechanics.

Human beings are highly predictable as physico-chemical systems, less predictable as living bodies, much less so as conscious beings and hardly at all as self-aware persons. The reason for this unpredictability does not lie in a lack of *adaequatio* on the part of the investigator, but in the nature of freedom. In the face of freedom, 'knowledge for manipulation' is impossible; but 'knowledge for understanding' is indispensable. The almost complete disappearance of the latter from Western civilisation is due to nothing but the systematic neglect of traditional wisdom, of which the West has as rich a store as any other part of mankind. The result of the lopsided development of the last three hundred years is that Western man is rich in means and poor in ends. The hierarchy of his knowledge has been decapitated; his will is paralysed because he has lost any grounds on which to base a hierarchy of values. What are his highest values?

A man's highest values are reached when he claims that

something is a good in itself, requiring no justification in terms of any higher good. Modern society prides itself on its 'pluralism', which means that a large number of things are admissible as 'good in themselves', as ends rather than means to an end. They are all of equal rank, all to be accorded first priority. If something that requires no justification may be called an 'absolute', the modern world, which claims that everything is relative, does in fact worship a very large number of 'absolutes'. It would be impossible to compile a complete list, and we shall not attempt it here. Not only power and wealth are treated as good in themselves—provided they are mine, and not someone else's—but also knowledge for its own sake, speed of movement, size of market, rapidity of change, quantity of education, number of hospitals, etc. In truth, none of these sacred cows is a genuine end: they are all means parading as ends. 'In the *Inferno* of the world of knowledge,' comments Etienne Gilson,

> there is a special punishment for this sort of sin; it is a relapse into mythology ... A world which has lost the Christian God cannot but resemble a world which had not yet found him. Just like the world of Thales and of Plato, our modern world is 'full of gods'. There are blind Evolution, clear-sighted Orthogenesis, benevolent Progress, and others which it is more advisable not to name. Why unnecessarily hurt the feelings of men who, today, render them a cult? It is however important for us to realise that mankind is doomed to live more and more under the spell of a new scientific, social, and political mythology, unless we resolutely exorcise these befuddled notions whose influence on modern life is becoming appalling ... For when gods fight among themselves, men have to die.[6]

When there are so many gods, all competing with one another and claiming first priority, and there is no supreme god, no supreme good or value, in terms of which everything else needs to justify itself, society cannot but drift into chaos. The modern world is full of people whom Gilson describes as 'pseudo-agnostics who ... combine scientific knowledge and social generosity with a complete lack of philosophical culture';[7] they ruthlessly use the prestige of 'science for manipulation' to discourage people from trying to restore wholeness to the edifice of human knowledge by developing— re-developing—a 'science for understanding'. Is it fear that motivates them? Abraham Maslow suggests that the pursuit of science is often a defence. 'It can be primarily a safety philosophy, a security system, a complicated way of avoiding anxiety and upsetting problems. In the extreme instance it can be a way of avoiding life, a kind of self-cloistering.'[8] However that may be, and it is not our task and purpose to study the psychology of scientists, there is undoubtedly also an urgent desire to escape from any traditional notions of human duties, responsibilities or obligations the neglect of which may be sinful. In spite of the modern world's chaos and its suffering, there is hardly a concept more unacceptable to it than the idea of sin. What could be the meaning of sin anyhow? Tradition says it means 'missing the mark', as in archery; missing the very purpose of human life on earth, a life that affords unique opportunities for development, a great chance and privilege, as the Buddhists have it, 'hard to obtain'. Whether tradition speaks the truth or not cannot be decided by any 'science for manipulation': it can be decided only by the highest faculties of man that are *adequate* to the creation of a 'science for under- standing'. If the very possibility of the latter is systematically denied, the highest faculties are never brought into play; they atrophy, and the very possibility of first understanding and then fulfilling the purpose of life disappears.

William James was under no illusion on the point that this matter, for each of us, is primarily a question of our will—as indeed faith is seen traditionally as a matter of the will.

> The question of having moral beliefs at all or not having them, is decided by our will. Are our moral preferences true or false, or are they only odd biological phenomena, making things good or bad for *us*, but in themselves indifferent? How can your pure intellect decide? If your heart does not *want* a world of moral reality, your head will assuredly never make you believe in one. Mephisto- phelian scepticism, indeed, will satisfy the head's play- instincts much better than any rigorous idealism can.[9]

The modern world tends to be sceptical about everything that demands man's higher faculties. But it is not at all sceptical about scepticism, which demands hardly anything.

6

The Four Fields of Knowledge

—FIELD ONE

The first landmark we have chosen for the construction of our philosophical map and guidebook is the hierarchic structure of the world—four great Levels of Being where the higher level always 'comprehends' the levels below it.

The second landmark is the similar structure of human senses, abilities, cognitive powers—similar in the sense of 'corresponding', for we cannot experience any part or facet of the world unless we possess and use an organ or instrument through which we can receive what is being offered. If we do not have the requisite organ or instrument, or if we fail to use it, we are not *adequate* to this particular part or facet of the world with the result that, as far as we are concerned, it simply does not exist. This is the great truth of *adaequatio*.

It follows from this truth that any systematic neglect or restriction in the use of our organs of cognition must inevitably have the effect of making the world appear less meaningful, rich, interesting, etc., than it actually is, while the opposite is equally true: the use of organs of cognition which for one reason or another normally lie dormant, and their systematic development and perfection, enable us to discover new meaning, new riches, new interest—facets of the world that had previously been inaccessible to us.

We have seen that the modern sciences, in a determined effort to attain objectivity and precision, have indeed restricted the use of the human instruments of cognition in a somewhat extreme way: according to some scientific interpreters, to observations by colour-blind, non-stereoscopic vision against quantitative scales. Such a methodology would necessarily

73

produce a picture of the world virtually confined to the lowest
level of manifestation, that of inanimate matter, and would
tend to suggest that the higher Levels of Being, including
human beings, were really nothing other than atoms in somewhat complex arrangements. We shall now have to pursue
this matter a little further. If the current methodology produces
an incomplete, one-sided and grossly impoverished picture,
what methods would need to be applied to obtain the full
picture?

It has often been observed that for every one of us reality
splits into two parts: here is I; and there is everything else, the
world, including you.

We have also had occasion to observe another duality: there
are visibilities and invisibilities or, we might say: outer
appearances and inner experiences. The latter become
relatively more and more important, as against the former, as
we move up the Great Chain of Being. Inner experiences
unquestionably exist, but they cannot be observed by our
ordinary senses.

From these two pairs—
   'I' and 'the World'
   'Outer Appearance' and 'Inner Experience'—
we obtain four 'combinations' which we can indicate thus:

  (1) I—inner   (3) I—outer
  (2) the world (you) inner   (4) the world (you) outer.

These are *the four fields of knowledge*, each of which is of great
interest and importance to every one of us. The four questions
that lead to these fields of knowledge may be put like this:

  (1) What is really going on in my own inner world?
  (2) What is going on in the inner world of other beings?
  (3) What do I look like in the eyes of other beings?
  (4) What do I actually observe in the world around me?

To simplify in an extreme manner we might say:

  (1) = What do I feel like?
  (2) = What do you feel like?
  (3) = What do I look like?
  (4) = What do you look like?

(The numbering of these four questions, and consequently of
the four fields of knowledge, is of course quite arbitrary.)

Now, the first point to make about these four fields of

knowledge is that we have direct access to only two of them—field (1) and field (4); that is to say, I can directly feel what I feel like, and I can directly see what you look like; but what it feels like to be you, I cannot directly know; and what I look like in your eyes, I do not know either. How we obtain knowledge of the other two fields—(2) and (3)—which are *not* directly accessible to us, i.e. how we come to know and understand what is going on inside other beings (field 2) and what we ourselves are from the outside, simply as an object of observation, as one being among countless other beings (field 3): how we enter these two fields of knowledge is indeed one of the most interesting, and also vital, questions that can be posed.

Socrates (in Plato's *Phaedrus*) says: 'I must first know myself, as the Delphian inscription says; to be curious about that which is not my concern, while I am still in ignorance of my own self, would be ridiculous.' Let us follow this example and start with *field of knowledge* (1)—what, really is going on inside myself; what gives me joy, what gives me pain? What strengthens me and what weakens me? Where do I control life and where does life control me? Am I in control of my mind, my feelings, can I do what I want to do? What is the value of this inner knowledge for the conduct of my life?

Before we go into any details we should take cognisance of the fact that the above-quoted statement from Plato's *Phaedrus* can be matched by similar statements from all parts of the world and all times. A whole book could be filled with relevant quotations. I shall confine myself to taking a few from the collection made by Mr Whitall N. Perry.[1]

Philo the Jew (late first century B.C.):

> For pray do not ... spin your airy fables about moon or sun or the other objects in the sky and in the universe so far removed from us and so varied in their natures, until you have scrutinised and come to know yourselves. After that, we may perhaps believe you when you hold forth on other subjects; but before you establish who you yourselves are, do not think that you will ever become capable of acting as judges or trustworthy witnesses in the other matters.

Plotinus (d. A.D. 270):

> Withdraw into yourself and look. And if you do not find yourself beautiful yet, act as does the creator of a statue that is to be made beautiful; he cuts away here, he smoothes there, he makes this line lighter, this other purer, until a lovely face has grown upon his work. So do you also: ... never cease chiselling your statue ...

Theologia Germanica (*c.* A.D. 1350):

> Thoroughly to know oneself, is above all art, for it is the highest art. If thou knowest thyself well, thou art better and more praiseworthy before God, than if thou didst not know thyself, but didst understand the course of the heavens and of all the planets and stars, also the virtue of all herbs, and the structure and dispositions of all mankind, also the nature of all beasts, and, in such matters, hadst all the skill of all who are in heaven and on earth.

And what did Paracelsus (1493?–1541) say, who was one of the most knowledgeable men of his time and foremost in knowing 'the virtue of all herbs'?

> Men do not know themselves, and therefore they do not understand the things of their inner world. Each man has the essence of God and all the wisdom and power of the world (germinally) in himself; he possesses one kind of knowledge as much as another, and he who does not find that which is in him cannot truly say that he does not possess it, but only that he was not capable of successfully seeking for it.

From India, Swami Ramdas (1886–1963):

> 'Seek within—know thyself', these secret and sublime hints come to us wafted from the breath of Rishis through the dust of ages.

From the world of Islam; Azid ibn Muhammad al-Nasafi (seventh–eighth century A.D.):

> When Ali asked Mohammad, 'What am I to do that I may not waste my time?' the Prophet answered, 'Learn to know thyself.'

And from China: the *Tao Te Ching* by Lao-Tzu (*c.* 604–531 B.C.):

> He who knows others is wise;
> He who knows himself is enlightened.

Many of Shakespeare's plays are entirely about the process of gaining self-knowledge, particularly *Measure for Measure*:

> I pray you, sir, of what disposition was the duke?
> One that, above all other strifes, contended especially to know himself.[2]

Finally, let us listen to a twentieth-century writer, P. D. Ouspensky (1878–1947), who states his 'fundamental idea' as follows:

> ... that man as we know him *is not a completed being*; that nature develops him only up to a certain point and then leaves him, either to develop further, *by his own* efforts and devices, or to live and die such as he was born, or to degenerate and lose capacity for development.
>
> Evolution of man ... will mean the development of certain *inner* qualities and features which usually remain undeveloped, *and cannot develop by themselves*.[3]

The modern world knows little of all this, even though it produces more psychological theories and literature than any previous age had done. As Ouspensky says, 'Psychology is sometimes called a new science. This is quite wrong. Psychology is, perhaps, the *oldest science*, and, unfortunately, in its most essential features a *forgotten science*.'[4] These 'most essential features' had presented themselves primarily in religious teachings, and their disappearance is largely accounted for by the decline of religions during the last few centuries.

Traditional psychology, which saw people as 'pilgrims' and 'wayfarers' on this earth who could reach the summit of a mountain of 'salvation', 'enlightenment' or 'liberation', was not primarily concerned with sick people who had to be made 'normal', but with normal people who were capable of becoming, and indeed destined to become, supernormal. Many of the great traditions have the idea of 'the way' at their very centre; the Chinese teaching of Taoism is named after *tao*, the Way; the Buddha's teaching is called 'The Middle Way', and

Jesus Christ Himself declares: 'I am the Way.' It is the pilgrim's task to undertake a journey into the interior, which demands a degree of heroism and in any case a readiness occasionally to turn one's back on the petty preoccupations of everyday life. As Joseph Campbell shows in his wonderful study of *The Hero with a Thousand Faces*, the traditional teachings, most of which are in the form of mythology, do 'not hold as [their] greatest hero the merely virtuous man. Virtue is but the pedagogical prelude to the culminating insight, which goes beyond all pairs of opposites.'[5] Only a perfectly clean instrument can obtain a perfectly clear picture.

It should not be thought that the 'journey into the interior' is only for heroes. It requires an inner commitment; and there is something heroic about any commitment to the unknown, but it is a heroism within everybody's capability. It is obvious that the study of this 'first field of knowledge' demands the whole person, for only a whole person can be adequate to the task. A one-eyed, colour-blind observer certainly would not get very far. But how can the whole person—particularly the human being's highest qualities—be brought into play? When discussing the Four Levels of Being we found that the enormous superiority of the human over the animal level needed to be acknowledged; and the 'additional power'—'z'—which accounted for man's superiority over the animals, we identified as being closely connected with *self-awareness*. Without self-awareness, the exploration and study of the inner man, i.e. one's interior world, is completely impossible.

Now, self-awareness is closely related to the power of attention, or perhaps I should say to the power of *directing* attention. My attention is often or even most of the time captured by outside forces which I may or may not have chosen myself—sounds, colours, etc.— or else by forces inside myself— expectations, fears, worries, interests, etc. When it is so captured, I function very much like a machine; I am not doing things: they simply happen. All the time there is, however, the possibility that I might take the matter in hand, and quite freely and deliberately direct my attention to something entirely of my own choosing, something that does not capture me but is to be captured by me. The difference between directed and captured attention is the same as the difference between doing things and letting things take their course, or between living and 'being lived'. No subject could be of greater interest; no subject occupies a more central place in all traditional teachings; and no subject suffers more neglect, misunderstanding and distortion in the thinking of the modern world.

In his book on *Yoga*, Ernest Wood talks about a state which he (wrongly, I believe) calls contemplation. He says:

> Yes, we often 'lose ourselves'. We peep into someone's office or study, and tip-toe away, whispering to our companions, 'He is lost in thought.' I knew a man who used to lecture frequently, on subjects requiring much thought. He told me that he had acquired the power to put himself out of mind—completely forget himself—at the commencement of a lecture, and look mentally at his subject-matter like a map on which he was following a route, while the spoken words flowed in complete obedience to the successive ideas which were being looked at. He told me that he would become aware of himself perhaps once or twice during the lecture, and at the end of it, as he sat down, he would find himself surprised that it was he who had given the lecture. Yet he fully remembered everything.[6]

This is a very good description of a man acting like a programmed machine, implementing a programme devised some time ago. *He*, the programmer, is no longer needed; he can mentally absent himself. If the machine is implementing a good programme it gives a good lecture; if the programme is bad, the lecture is bad. We are all very familiar with the possibility of implementing 'programmes', e.g. when driving a car and engaging in an interesting conversation at the same time. Paradoxically, we may be driving 'attentively', carefully, considerately, yet all our real attention is with the conversation. Are we equally familiar with directing our attention to where we want it to be, not depending on any 'attraction', and keeping it there for as long as we desire? The truth of the matter is that we are not. Such moments of full freedom and self-awareness are all too rare. Most of our life is spent in some kind of thraldom; we are captivated by this or that, are drifting along in our captivity, and we carry out programmes that have been lodged in our machine, we do not know how, when or by whom.

The first subject for study in what I have called 'field one' is therefore *attention*, and this leads immediately to a study of our mechanicalness. The best help in this study that I know of is P. D. Ouspensky's book, *The Psychology of Man's Possible Evolution*.

It is not difficult to verify for oneself Ouspensky's observation that we may at any time find ourselves in any one of three different 'states' or 'parts of ourselves'—mechanical, emotional or intellectual (to use his terminology). The chief criterion for identifying these different 'parts' is the quality of our attention.

> Without attention or with attention wandering, we are in the mechanical part; with the attention attracted by the subject of observation or reflection and kept there, we are in the emotional part; with the attention controlled and held on the subject by will, we are in the intellectual part.[7]

Now, in order to be aware of where our attention is and what it is doing, we have to be *awake* in a rather exacting meaning of the word. When we are acting or thinking or feeling mechanically, like a programmed computer or any other machine, we are obviously not awake in that sense, and we are doing, thinking or feeling things that we have not ourselves freely chosen to do, think or feel. We may say afterwards: 'I did not mean to do it' or 'I don't know what came over me.' We may intend, undertake and even solemnly promise to do all kinds of things, but if we are at any time liable to drift into actions 'we did not mean to do' or to be pushed by some thing that 'comes over us', what is the value of our intentions? When we are not awake in our attention, we are certainly not self-aware and therefore not fully human; we are likely to act helplessly in accordance with uncontrolled inner drives or outer compulsions, like animals.

Mankind did not have to wait for the arrival of modern psychology to obtain teachings on these vitally important matters. Traditional wisdom, including all the great religions, as mentioned before, has always described itself as 'The Way' and given some kind of awakening as the goal. Buddhism has been called the 'Doctrine of Awakening'. Throughout the New Testament, people are admonished to stay awake, to watch, not to fall asleep. At the beginning of the *Divine Comedy*, Dante finds himself in a dark wood, and he does not know how he got there: '*so full was I of slumber at that moment when I abandoned the true way.*' It is not physical sleep that is the enemy of man; it is the drifting, wandering, shiftless moving of his attention that makes man incompetent, miserable and less-than-fully-human. Without self-awareness, i.e. without a consciousness that is conscious of itself, man merely imagines that he is in control of himself, that he has free will and is able to carry out his intentions. In fact, as Ouspensky would put it, he has no more freedom to form intentions and act in accordance with them than has a machine. Only in occasional moments of self-awareness has he such freedom, and his most important task is by one means or another to make self-awareness continuous and controllable.

For this purpose, different religions have evolved different ways. Here we can look only at a few examples. The 'heart of Buddhist meditation' is *satipatthana*, or mindfulness. One of the outstanding Buddhist monks of today, Nyanaponika Thera, introduces his book on this subject with these words:

> This book is issued in the deep conviction that the systematic cultivation of Right Mindfulness, as taught by the Buddha in his Discourse on Satipatthana, still provides the most simple and direct, the most thorough and effective, method for training the mind for its daily tasks and problems as well as for its highest aim: mind's unshakeable deliverance from Greed, Hatred and Delusion ...
>
> This ancient Way of Mindfulness is as practicable today as it was 2,500 years ago. It is applicable in the lands of the West as in the East; in the midst of life's turmoil as well as in the peace of the monk's cell.[8]

The essence of the development of Right Mindfulness is an increase in the intensity and quality of attention, and the essence of *quality* of attention is its *bareness*.

Bare attention is the clear and single-minded awareness of what actually happens *to* us and *in* us, at the successive moments of perception. It is called 'bare', because it attends just to the bare facts of a perception as presented ... Attention or mindfulness is kept to a bare registering of the facts observed, without reacting to them by deed, speech or by mental comment which may be one of self-reference (like, dislike, etc.), judgment or reflection. If during the time, short or long, given to the practice of Bare Attention, any such comments arise in one's mind, they themselves are made objects of Bare Attention, and are neither repudiated nor pursued, but are dismissed, after a brief mental note has been made of them.[9]

These few indications may suffice to identify the essential nature of the method: Bare Attention is attainable only by stopping or, if it cannot be stopped, calmly observing all 'inner chatter'. It stands *above* thinking, reasoning, arguing, forming opinions — those essential yet subsidiary activities that classify, connect and verbalise the insights obtained through Bare Attention. 'In employing the methods of Bare Attention', says Nyanaponika, the mind 'goes back to the seed state of things ... Observation reverts to the very first phase of the process of perception when mind is in a purely receptive state, and when attention is restricted to a bare noticing of the object.'[10]

In the words of the Buddha, 'In what is seen there must be only the seen; in what is heard there must be only the heard; in what is sensed (as smell, taste or touch) there must be only what is sensed; in what is thought there must be only what is thought.'[11]

In short, the Buddha's Way of Mindfulness is designed to ensure that man's reason is supplied with genuine and un-adulterated material before it starts reasoning. What is it that tends to adulterate the material? Obviously, man's egoism, his attachment to interests, desires or, in Buddhist language, his greed, hatred and delusion.

Religion is the re-connection (*re-legio*) of man with reality, whether this reality be called God, Truth, Allah, Sat-Chit-Ananda or Nirvana. The methods evolved in the Christian tradition are clothed, not surprisingly, in a very different vocabulary, but they none the less come to the same. Nothing can be achieved or attained as long as the little egocentric 'I' stands in the way—there may in fact be many little, egocentric and quite unco-ordinated 'I's—and to get away from the 'I', man must attend to 'God'—with 'naked intent', as a famous English classic, *The Cloud of Unknowing*, calls it: 'A naked intention directed to God, and himself alone, is wholly sufficient.' The enemy is the intervention of *thought*.

> Should any thought arise and obtrude itself between you and the darkness, asking what you are seeking, and what you are wanting, answer that it is God you want: 'Him I covet, him I seek, and nothing but him.' ... Quite possibly he [the thought] will bring to your mind many lovely and wonderful thoughts of his kindness ... He will go on chattering increasingly ... [and] your mind will be well away, back in its old haunts. Before you know where you are you are disintegrated beyond belief! And the reason? Simply that you freely consented to listen to that thought, and responded to it, accepted it, and gave it its head.[12]

It is not a question of good or bad thoughts. Reality, Truth, God, Nirvana cannot be found by thought, because thought belongs to the Level of Being established by consciousness and not to that higher Level which is established by self-awareness. At the latter, thought has its legitimate place, but it is a sub-servient one. Thoughts cannot lead to 'Awakening' because the whole point is to awake from thinking into 'seeing'. Thought can raise any number of questions; they may all be interesting, but their answers do nothing to wake us up. In Buddhism, they are called 'vain thoughts':

> This is called the blind alley of opinions, the gorge of opinions, the bramble of opinions, the thicket of opinions, the net of opinions ... Opinion, O disciples, is a disease; opinion is a tumour; opinion is a sore. He who has over-come all opinion, O disciples, is called a saint, one who knows.[13]

What is yoga? According to the greatest of yoga teachers, Patanjali (around 300 B.C.), 'Yoga is the control of the ideas in the mind.' Our circumstances are not merely the facts of life as we meet them, but also, and even more, the ideas in our minds. It is impossible to obtain any control over circumstances without first obtaining control over the ideas in one's mind, and the most important—as well as the most universal—teaching of all the religions is that *vipassana* (to use a Buddhist term), the clarity of vision, can be attained only by him who succeeds in putting the 'thinking function' in its place, so that it maintains silence when ordered to do so and moves into action only when given a definite and specific task. Here is another quotation from *The Cloud of Unknowing*:

> Therefore the vigorous working of your imagination, which is always so active ... must as often be suppressed. *Unless you suppress it, it will suppress you.*[14]

While the centrepiece of the Indian method is yoga, the centrepiece of the Christian method is prayer. To ask God for help, to thank Him and to praise Him are legitimate purposes of Christian prayer; all the same, the essence of prayer goes beyond this. The Christian is called upon to 'pray without ceasing'. Jesus 'spake a parable unto them to this end, that men ought always to pray, and not to faint' (Luke XVIII.1). This command has engaged the most serious attention of Christians throughout the centuries. Perhaps the most famous passage on it is found in *The Candid Narrations of a Pilgrim to His Spiritual Father*, an anonymous jewel of world literature which was first printed in Russia in 1884.

> The first Epistle of St. Paul to the Thessalonians was read. In it we are exhorted, among other things, to *pray* incessantly, and these words engraved themselves upon my mind. I began to ponder whether it is possible to pray without ceasing, since every man must occupy himself with other things needed for his support ... 'What am I to do?' I mused. 'Where will I be able to find someone who can explain it to me?'[15]

The pilgrim then obtains the *Philokalia*,[16] which 'comprises the complete and minute knowledge of incessant inner prayer, as stated by twenty-five Holy Fathers'.

This inner prayer is also called 'prayer of the heart'; while by no means unknown in the West, it has been brought to perfection mainly in the Greek and Russian Orthodox Churches. The essence of it is 'standing before God with the mind in the heart'. This has been explained as follows:

> The term 'heart' is of particular significance in the Orthodox doctrine of man. When people in the west today speak of the heart, they usually mean the emotions and affections. But in the Bible, as in most ascetic texts of the Orthodox Church, the heart has a far wider connotation. It is the primary organ of man's being, whether physical or spiritual; it is the centre of life, the determining principle of all our activities and aspirations. As such, the heart obviously includes the affections and emotions, but it also includes much else besides: it embraces in effect everything that goes to comprise what we call a 'person'.[17]

Now, the *person* is distinguished from other beings by the mysterious power of self-awareness and this power, as we have already noted, has its seat in the heart, where, in fact, it can be felt as a peculiar kind of warmth. The prayer of the heart, normally the Jesus Prayer (consisting in English of these words: 'Lord Jesus Christ, son of God, have mercy upon me, a sinner') is endlessly repeated by the mind *in the heart*, and this vitalises, moulds and reforms the whole person. One of the great teachers of this matter, Theophan the Recluse (1815–94), explains thus:

> In order to keep the mind on one thing by the use of a short prayer, it is necessary to preserve attention and so lead it into the heart: for so long as the mind remains in the head, where thoughts jostle one another, it has no time to concentrate on one thing. But when attention descends into the heart, it attracts all the powers of the soul and body into one point there. This concentration of all human life in one place is immediately reflected in the heart by a special sensation that is the beginning of future warmth. This sensation, faint at the beginning, becomes gradually stronger, firmer, deeper. At first only tepid, it grows into warm feeling and concentrates the attention upon itself. And so it comes about that, whereas in the initial stages the attention is kept in the heart by an

effort of will, in due course this attention, by its own vigour, gives birth to warmth in the heart. This warmth then holds the attention without special effort. From this, the two go on supporting one another, and must remain inseparable; because dispersion of attention cools the warmth, and diminishing warmth weakens attention.[18]

The assertion that the endless repetition, silently, of a short sequence of words leads to a spiritual result, signalised, as it were, by *physical* sensations of *spiritual* warmth, is so strange to the modern mentality that it tends to be dismissed as mumbo-jumbo. Our pragmatism and respect for facts, of which we are so immensely proud, does not easily induce us to try it. Why not? Because trying it leads to the acquisition of certain insights, certain types of knowledge, that, once we have opened ourselves to them, will not leave us alone: they will present a kind of ultimatum — either you change or you perish. The modern world likes matters to trifle with; but the results of a direct approach to the study and development of self-awareness are not to be trifled with.

The First Field of Knowledge, in other words, is a minefield for anyone who fails to recognise that, at the human Level of Being, the '*invisibilia*' are of infinitely greater power and significance than the '*visibilia*'. To teach this basic truth has traditionally been the function of religion, and since religion has been abandoned by Western civilisation nothing remains to provide this teaching. Western civilisation, consequently, has become incapable of dealing with the real problems of life at the human Level of Being. Its competence at the lower levels is breathtakingly powerful; but when it comes to the essentially human concerns it is both ignorant and incompetent. Without the wisdom and disciplines of authentic religion, the first field of knowledge remains neglected, a wasteland overgrown with weeds, many of them poisonous. Healthy and useful plants may still appear there, but only, as it were, accidentally. Without self-awareness (in the full sense of 'factor z') man acts, speaks, studies, reacts mechanically, like a machine: on the basis of 'programmes' acquired accidentally, unintentionally, mechanically. He is not aware that he is acting in accordance with programmes; it is therefore not difficult to re-programme him—to make him think and do quite different things from those he had thought and done before—provided only that the new programme does not wake him up. When he is awake, no one can programme him: he programmes himself.

This ancient teaching, which I am merely expressing in modern terms, implies that there are two elements or agents involved rather than one—the computer programmer and the computer. The latter functions perfectly well without the attention of the former—as a machine. Consciousness—'factor y'—functions perfectly well without the presence of self-awareness, 'factor z', as is demonstrated by all higher animals. That the fullness of the human 'mind' cannot be accounted for by only one element is the universal assertion of all the great religions, an assertion that has recently been corroborated by modern science. Just before his death at the age of eighty-four, Dr Wilder Penfield, world-famous neurologist and brain surgeon, published a *summa* of his findings under the title *The Mystery of the Mind*. He says:

> Throughout my own scientific career, I, like other scientists, have struggled to prove that the brain accounts for the mind. But now, perhaps, the time has come when we may profitably consider the evidence as it stands, and ask the question: *Do brain mechanisms account for the mind?* Can the mind be explained by what is now known about the brain? If not, which is the more reasonable of the two possible hypotheses: that man's being is based on one element, or on two?[19]

Dr Penfield comes to the conclusion that 'the mind seems to act independently of the brain in the same sense that a programmer acts independently of his computer, however much he may depend upon the action of that computer for certain purposes.' He goes on to explain:

> Because it seems to me certain that it will always be quite impossible to explain the mind on the basis of neuronal action within the brain, and because it seems to me that the mind develops and matures independently throughout an individual's life as though it were a continuing element, and because a computer (which the brain is) must be

operated by an agency capable of independent understanding, I am forced to choose the proposition that our being is to be explained on the basis of two fundamental elements.[20]

Obviously, the programmer is 'higher' than the computer, just as what I have called self-awareness is 'higher' than consciousness. Studying the first field of knowledge implies the systematic training of the 'higher' factor. The programmer cannot be trained simply by letting the computer run more regularly or faster. His requirement is not simply knowledge of facts and theories, but understanding or *insight*. Not surprisingly, the processes of gaining insight are quite different from those of gaining factual knowledge. Many people are incapable of seeing the difference between knowledge and insight and therefore view methods of training like *satipatthana*, yoga or unceasing prayer as some kind of superstitious nonsense. Such views are of course quite valueless and merely indicate a lack of *adaequatio*. All systematic effort produces some kind of result.

The Jesus Prayer acts as a constant reminder to make man look inwards *at all times*, to become aware of his fleeting thoughts, sudden emotions and even movements so that it may make him try to control them ... By scrutinising and observing his own inner self he will obtain an increasing knowledge of his worthlessness which may fill him with despair ... These are the birth pangs of the spirit and the groanings of awakening spirituality in man ... One is advised to repeat the prayer of Jesus in 'silence'. Silence here is meant to include inner silence; the silence of one's own mind, the arresting of the imagination from the ever-turbulent and ever-present stream of thoughts, words, impressions, pictures and day-dreams, which keep one asleep. This is not easy, as the mind works almost autonomously.[21]

Few Western philosophers of the modern age have given serious attention to the methods of studying the first field of knowledge. A rare exception is W. T. Stace, for about twenty-five years, from 1935, a professor of philosophy at Princeton

University. In his book, *Mysticism and Philosophy*[22] he asks the long overdue question: 'What bearing, if any, does what is called "mystical experience" have upon the more important problems of philosophy?', and his investigations lead him to 'the introvertive type of mystical experience', and thus to the methods employed by those seeking such experiences. It is perhaps unfortunate that Professor Stace uses the word 'mystical', which has acquired a somewhat *mystical* meaning, when in fact nothing other is involved than the attentive exploration of one's own inner life. However, this does not detract from the pertinence and excellence of his observations.

First of all, he points out that *there is no doubt* that the basic psychological facts about this 'introvertive experience' are in essence 'the same all over the world in all cultures, religions, places, and ages'. Professor Stace writes as a philosopher and does not claim to have any personal experience of these matters. He therefore finds them very strange indeed. 'They are', he says, 'so extraordinary and paradoxical that they are bound to strain belief when suddenly sprung upon anyone who is not prepared for them.' He then proceeds to set forth 'the alleged facts as the mystics state them without comment and without passing judgment'. Although he states the facts in terms which no mystic has ever used, his method of exposition is so clear that it is worth reproducing here in summary form:

Suppose that one should stop up the inlets of the physical senses so that no sensations could reach consciousness ... There seems to be no *a priori* reason why a man bent on the goal ... should not, by acquiring sufficient concentration and mental control, exclude all physical sensations from his consciousness.

Suppose that, after having got rid of all sensations, one should go on to exclude from consciousness all sensuous images and then all abstract thoughts, reasoning processes, volitions, and other particular contents; what would then be left of consciousness? There would be no mental content whatever but rather a complete emptiness, vacuum, void.[23]

This is, of course, precisely the aim pursued by those who wish to study their inner life: the exclusion of all disturbing influences emanating from the senses or from the 'thinking function'. Professor Stace, however, becomes deeply puzzled:

> One would suppose *a priori* that consciousness would then entirely lapse and one would fall asleep or become unconscious. But the introvertive mystics—thousands of them all over the world—unanimously assert that they have attained to this complete vacuum of particular mental contents, but what then happens is quite different from a lapse into unconsciousness. On the contrary, what emerges is a state of *pure* consciousness—'pure' in the sense that it is not the consciousness *of* any empirical content. It has no content except itself.[24]

In the language I used previously we might say: the computer programmer emerges who, of course, has none of the 'contents' of the computer; in other words, again, the factor z—self-awareness—really comes into its own when, and only when, the factor y—consciousness—leaves the centre of the stage. Professor Stace says: 'The paradox is that there should be a positive experience which has no positive content—an experience which is both something and nothing.'[25]

But there is nothing paradoxical in a 'higher' force displacing a 'lower' force, in an experience that is something but *no thing*. The paradox exists only for those who insist on believing that there can be nothing 'higher than' or 'above' their everyday consciousness and experience. How could they believe such a thing? Everybody, surely, has had some moments in his life which held more significance and real-ness of experience than his everyday life. Such moments are pointers, glimpses of unrealised potentialities, flashes of self-awareness. Professor Stace continues his exploration thus:

> Our normal everyday consciousness always has objects, or images, or even our own feelings or thoughts perceived introspectively. Suppose then that we obliterate all objects physical or mental. *When the self is not engaged in apprehending objects it becomes aware of itself.* The self itself emerges ...
>
> One may also say that the mystic gets rid of the empirical ego whereupon the pure ego, normally hidden,

emerges into the light. *The empirical ego is the stream of consciousness. The pure ego is the unity which holds the manifold of the stream together.*[26] [Italics are mine.]

The essential identity of these views with those of Dr Wilder Penfield is unmistakable. Both corroborate the central teaching of the great religions which, in many different languages and modes of expression, urge man to open himself to the 'pure ego' or 'Self' or 'Emptiness' or 'Divine Power' that dwells within him; to awake, as it were, out of the computer into the programmer; to transcend consciousness by self-awareness. Only by liberating oneself from the thraldom of the senses and the thinking function—both of them servants and not masters—by withdrawing attention from the *things seen* to give it to the *things unseen*—can this 'awakening' be accomplished. ' ... we look not at the things which are seen, but at the things which are not seen; for the things which are seen are temporal; but the things which are not seen are eternal' (2 Cor. IV.18).

There is a very great deal more that could be said about this greatest of all arts, the acquisition of self-knowledge, by, in our terminology, the study of the first field of knowledge. It will be more useful, however, now to turn to the *second field of knowledge*, that is the knowledge we may obtain of the *inner* experience of *other* beings. One thing is certain: We seem to have no direct access to such knowledge (as already mentioned). How then is such knowledge possible at all?

7

The Four Fields of Knowledge

—FIELD TWO

The higher the Level of Being, the greater is the importance of inner experience, i.e. the 'inner life', as compared with outer appearance, i.e. such measurable and directly observable attributes as size, weight, colour, movement, etc.; also, the more likely are we to be able to obtain some knowledge of the 'inner life' of other beings, at least up to the human level. We are convinced that we can indeed know something of what goes on inside another human being; a little bit even about the inner life of animals; virtually nothing about that of plants; and certainly nothing at all about that of stones and other pieces of inanimate matter. When St Paul says that 'We know that the whole creation groaneth and travaileth in pain together until now',[1] we can glimpse his meaning with regard to people and possibly animals but have very great difficulties when it comes to plants and minerals.

Let us then begin with other people. How do we gain knowledge of what is going on inside them? As I have said before, we are living in a world of *invisible* people; most of them do not even wish us to know anything about their inner life; they say, 'Don't intrude, leave me alone, mind your own business.' Even when somebody at some time wants to 'bare his soul' to someone else he finds it extraordinarily difficult to do so, does not know how to express himself and, without in the least wishing to mislead, tends to say many things that are not true at all; in desperation he may try to communicate without words— by gestures, signs, bodily touch, shouting, weeping, even violence.

Although there are constant temptations to forget it, we all know that our lives are made or marred by our relationships with other human beings; no amount of wealth, health, fame or power can compensate us for our losses if these relationships go wrong. Yet they all depend on our ability to understand others and their ability to understand us.

Most people seem to believe that there is nothing more to this problem of communication than listening to another person's speech and observing the outward movements of his body; in other words, that we can implicitly rely on other people's *visible* signals to convey to us a correct picture of their *invisible* thoughts, feelings, intentions, etc. Alas! the matter is not as simple as this. Consider the requirements step by step, assuming that there is a genuine wish on the part of one person to convey his thought to another person (and leaving out all possibilities of deliberate deceit).

—First, the speaker must know, with some precision, what *is* the thought he wishes to convey;

—second, he must find visible (including audible) symbols—gestures, bodily movements, words, intonation, etc.—which in his judgment are able to 'externalise' his 'internal' thought; this may be called '*the first translation*';

—third, the listener must have a faultless reception of these visible (etc.) symbols, which means not only that he must accurately hear what is being said, knowing the language used, but also that he must accurately observe the non-verbal symbols (such as gesture and intonation) that are being employed;

—fourth, the listener must then in some way integrate the numerous symbols he has received and turn them into thought; this may be called '*the second translation*'.

It is not difficult to see how much can go wrong at each stage of this four-stage process, particularly with the two 'translations'. In fact, we might come to the conclusion that reliable and accurate communication is impossible. Even if the speaker is completely clear about the thought he wishes to convey, his choice of symbols—gestures, word combinations, intonation—is a highly personal matter; and even if the listener listens and observes perfectly, how can he be sure that he attaches the appropriate meaning to the symbols he receives? These doubts and questions are only too well justified. The process, as described, is extremely laborious, and unreliable, even when immense time and effort is spent to formulate definitions, exceptions, provisos, explanations and escape clauses. We are immediately reminded of legal or international diplomatic documents. This, we might think, is a case of communication between two 'computers', where everything has to be reduced to pure logic: either–or. Here the dream of Descartes becomes real: nothing counts except precise, distinct and absolutely certain ideas.

All the same, miraculously, in real life perfect communication *is* possible, and is not infrequent. It proceeds without elaborate definitions or provisos or escape clauses. People are even capable of saying: 'I don't like the way you are putting it, but I agree with what you mean.' This is highly significant. There can be a 'meeting of minds', for which the words and gestures are little more than an invitation. Words, gestures, intonation: these can be one of two things (or even a bit of each) — computer language, or an invitation to two 'computer programmers' to get together.

If we cannot achieve a real 'meeting of minds' with the people nearest to us in our daily lives, our existence becomes an agony and a disaster. In order to achieve it, I must be able to gain knowledge of what it is like to be 'you'; and 'you' must be able to gain knowledge of what it is like to be me. Both of us must become knowledgeable in what I call the second field of knowledge. Since we know that only very little knowledge comes naturally to most of us and the acquisition of better knowledge requires effort, we are bound to ask ourselves the question: 'What can I do to acquire better knowledge, to become more understanding of what is going on inside the people with whom I live?'

Now, the remarkable fact is that all traditional teachings give one and the same answer to this question: 'You can understand other beings only to the extent that you know yourself.' Naturally, good observation and good listening are also necessary; the point is that even perfect observation and perfect listening lead to nothing unless the data thus obtained are correctly interpreted and understood, and the precondition of my ability to understand correctly is my own self-knowledge, my own inner experience. In other words, and using our previous terminology, there must be *adaequatio*, item by item, bit by bit. A person who had never consciously experienced bodily pain could not possibly know anything about pain suffered by others. The outward signs of pain—noises, movements, a flow of tears—would of course be noticed by him as by anyone else; but he would be totally *inadequate* to the task of understanding them correctly. No doubt he would attempt some kind of an interpretation; he might find them funny or menacing or simply incomprehensible. The 'invisibilia' of the other being—in this case his inner experience of pain—would remain invisible to him.

I leave it to the reader to explore the enormous range of inner experiences that fills the lives of men and women. As I have emphasised before, they are all invisible, inaccessible to external observation. The example of bodily pain is instructive precisely because there is no subtlety about it. Few people doubt the reality of pain, and the realisation that here is a thing that we all recognise as real, true, one of the great 'stubborn facts' of human existence, which none the less is *unobservable by our outer senses*, may come as a shock: if only that which can be observed by our outer senses is deemed to be real, 'objective', scientifically respectable, pain must be dismissed as unreal, 'subjective', unscientific. And the same applies to everything else that moves us internally—love and hatred, joy and sorrow, hope, fear, anguish, etc. If all these forces or movements inside me are not really real, they need not be taken seriously; and if I do not take them seriously in myself, how could I consider them real and take them seriously in another being? It is indeed more convenient to assume that other beings, including other people, do not really suffer as we do and do not really possess an inner life as complex, subtle and vulnerable as our own: throughout the ages, man has shown an enormous capacity to carry the sufferings of others with fortitude and equanimity. Since, moreover (as Mr J. G. Bennett has shrewdly observed),[2] we tend to see ourselves primarily in the light of our intentions, which are invisible to others, while we see others mainly in the light of their actions, which are visible to us, we have a situation in which misunderstandings and injustices are the order of the day.

There is no escape from this situation except by the diligent and systematic cultivation of the *first field of knowledge*, through which—and through which alone—we can obtain the insights needed for the cultivation of the second field of knowledge, i.e. knowledge of the inner experiences of other beings than ourselves.

To be able to take the inner life of my neighbour seriously, it is necessary that I should take my own inner life seriously. But what does that mean? It means that I must put myself in a condition so that I can truly observe what is going on and begin to understand what I observe. In modern times, there is no lack of understanding of the fact that man is a social being and 'no man is an Island, entire of itself' (John Donne, 1572–1631). Hence there is no lack of exhortation that he should love his neighbour, or at least not be nasty to him, and should practise tolerance, compassion and understanding. At the same time, however, the culture of self-knowledge has fallen into virtually total neglect, unless, that is to say, it is the object of active suppression. That you cannot love your neighbour unless you love yourself; that you cannot understand your neighbour unless you understand yourself; that there can be no knowledge of the 'invisible person' who is your neighbour except on the basis of self-knowledge—these fundamental truths are forgotten even by many of the professionals of the established religions.

Exhortations, consequently, cannot possibly have any effect; the place of genuine understanding of one's neighbour is taken by sentimentality which, of course, crumbles into nothingness as soon as self-interest is threatened and fear of any kind is aroused. The place of knowledge is taken by assumptions, trite theories, fantasies. The enormous popularity of the crudest and meanest psychological and economic doctrines purporting to 'explain' the actions and motives of others—never of ourselves! —shows the disastrous consequences of the current lack of competence in the second field of knowledge, which in turn is the direct result of the modern refusal to attend to the first field of knowledge, self-knowledge.

Anyone who openly goes on a 'journey into the interior' who withdraws from the ceaseless agitation of everyday life and pursues the kind of training—*sattipatthana*, yoga, Jesus Prayer or something similar — without which genuine self-knowledge cannot be obtained, is accused of selfishness and of turning his back on his social duties. Meanwhile, world crises multiply and everybody deplores the shortage, or even total lack, of 'wise' men or women, unselfish leaders, trustworthy counsellors. etc. It is hardly rational to expect such high qualities from people who have never done any *inner work*, and would not even understand what was meant by these words. They may consider themselves decent, law-abiding people and good citizens; maybe 'humanists', maybe 'believers'. It makes very little difference how they *dream* about themselves. Like a 'pianola', they play mechanical music; like a computer they carry out pre-arranged programmes. The programmer is asleep. An important part of the modern 'programme' is to reject religion as cheaply moralising, outdated, ceremonial dogmatism, thereby rejecting the very force, perhaps the only force, that could wake us up and lift us to the truly human level, that of self-awareness, self-control, self-knowledge and, thereby, of knowledge and understanding of others, and which would give us the power to help them when necessary.

People say: It is all a matter of communication. Of course it is. But communication, as mentioned before, implies two 'translations'—from thought to symbol and from symbol to thought. Symbols cannot be understood like mathematical formulae; they have to be experienced *interiorly*. They cannot properly be taken up by consciousness, but only by self-awareness. A gesture, for instance, cannot be understood by the rational mind; we have to become aware of its meaning inside ourselves, with our body rather than with our brain. Sometimes the only way to understand the mood or feelings of another person is by imitating his posture, gestures and facial expressions. There is a strange and mysterious connection between the interior-invisible and the exterior-visible. William James (1842–1910) was interested in the bodily expression of emotions and advanced the theory that the emotion we feel is nothing but the feeling of some bodily changes:

Common-sense says, we lose our fortune, are sorry and weep; we meet a bear, are frightened and run; we are insulted by a rival, are angry and strike. The hypothesis here to be defended says that this order of sequence is incorrect ... and that the more rational statement is that we feel sorry because we cry, angry because we strike, afraid because we tremble, and not that we cry, strike, or tremble, because we are sorry, angry, or fearful, as the case may be.[3]

The hypothesis, although probably more remarkable for its originality than for its truth value, brings into sharp focus the intimate connection between inner feeling and bodily expression; it points to a mysterious bridge connecting the invisible and the visible, and identifies the body as an *instrument of knowledge*. I have no doubt that a baby learns a great deal about its mother's emotions by imitating her posture and facial movements and then discovering what feelings are associated with these bodily expressions.

It is for these reasons that all methods devised for the acquisition of self-knowledge (field one) pay a great deal of attention to bodily postures and gestures; for the establishment of control over the body is, to say the least, the first step in the establishment of control over the thinking function. Uncontrolled agitation of the body inevitably produces uncontrollable agitation of the mind, a condition that precludes all serious study of one's inner world.

When a high degree of inner calmness and quietude has been established, the 'computer' is left behind and the 'computer programmer' comes into his own. In Buddhist terms, this is called *vipassana*, or 'clarity of vision'. In Christian terms, there is some kind of encounter with a higher Level of Being, above the human level. Naturally, those of us who have no personal experience of this higher level cannot imagine it, and the language of those who are trying to tell us about it either means nothing to us or appears to indicate a disordered mind, even madness. We have no easy means of distinguishing between infra-human and supra-human 'madness'. But we can look at the whole life of the person in question. If there is plenty of evidence of great intellectual powers, organising ability, wisdom and personal influence, we can be quite certain, when we cannot understand them, that

> The fault, dear Brutus, is not in our stars,
> But in ourselves, that we are underlings.

No one is *adequate* to that which lies above him, although an inkling and intimation of possibilities and an inspiration towards a real effort of awakening can always be obtained.

There is today a great deal of talk about the attainment of 'higher states of consciousness'. Unfortunately, this aspiration, in most cases, does not grow out of a deep respect for the great wisdom traditions of mankind, the world religions, but is based on fantastic notions of 'Aquarian Frontier' and 'Evolution of Consciousness', and associated with a total inability to distinguish between the spiritual and the occult. It seems that the real aim is to obtain new thrills, to master magic and miracles, thereby to enliven existential boredom. The advice of all people knowledgeable in these matters is *not* to seek occult experiences and *not* to pay any attention to them when they occur — and they almost inevitably *will* occur when any intensive inner work is undertaken. The great teacher of Buddhist Satipatthana Meditation, the Venerable Mahasi Sayadaw (1904–55), warns the pupil that he will have all sorts of extraordinary experiences:

> A brilliant light will appear to him. To one it will appear like the light of a lamp, to others like a flash of lightning, or like the radiance of the moon or the sun, and so on. With one it may last for just one moment, with others it may last longer ... There arises also *rapture* ... *tranquillity* of mind, ... a very sublime feeling of *happiness* ... Having felt such rapture and happiness accompanied by the 'brilliant light' ... the meditator now believes: 'Surely I must have attained to the Supra-mundane Path and Fruition! Now I have finished the task of meditation.' This is mistaking what is not the Path for the Path, and it is a corruption of Insight which usually takes place in the manner just described ... After noticing these manifestations of Brilliant Light and the others, or after leaving them unheeded, he [the true seeker] goes on continuously as before ... he gets over the corruptions relating to brilliant light, rapture, tranquillity, happiness, attachment, etc. ... [4]

Christian saints and sages are equally clear on this point. We can take St John of the Cross (1542–91) as a typical example:

> With respect to all [bodily senses] there may come, and there are wont to come, to spiritual persons representations and objects of a supernatural kind ...
>
> And it must be known that, although all these things may happen to the bodily senses in the way of God, *we must never rely upon them or accept them*, but must always fly from them, without trying to ascertain whether they be good or evil; ... for the bodily sense is as ignorant of spiritual things as is a beast of rational things, and even more so.
>
> So he that esteems such things *errs greatly and exposes himself to great peril of being deceived*; in any case he will have within himself a *complete impediment to the attainment of spirituality*.[5] [Italics are mine.]

The New Consciousness that is so much talked about today cannot help us out of our difficulties and will merely increase the prevailing confusion, unless it arises from a genuine search for self-knowledge (the first field of knowledge) and moves on to an equally genuine study of the inner life of other beings (the second field of knowledge) and also to the third field of knowledge, which will be discussed later. If it merely leads to fascination with occult phenomena, it belongs to the *fourth* field of knowledge (also to be considered later), and can do nothing to improve our understanding of ourselves and of our fellow creatures.

Inner work, or yoga in its many forms, is not a peculiarity of the East, but the taproot, as it were, of all authentic religions. It has been called 'the applied psychology of religion',[6] and it must be said that religion without applied psychology is completely worthless. 'Simply to believe a religion to be true, and to give intellectual assent to its creed and dogmatic theology, and not to know it to be true through having tested it by the scientific methods of yoga, results in the blind leading the blind.'[7] This statement comes from Dr W. Y. Evans-Wentz, who spent most of his life 'editing' sacred writings from Tibet and making them available to the West. He asks:

Is Occidental man for much longer to be content with the study of the external universe, and not know himself? If, as the editor believes, the Oriental sage is able to direct us of the Occident to a method of attaining scientific understanding of the hidden side of man's nature, are we not unwise in failing to give it unprejudiced scientific examination?

Applied sciences in our portion of the world are, unfortunately, limited to chemistry, economics, mathematics, mechanics, physics, physiology, and the like; and anthropology and psychology as applied sciences in the sense understood in *yoga* are for almost all Occidental scientists mere dreams of impracticable visionaries. We do not believe, however, that this unsound view can long endure.[8]

'Applied science in the sense understood in *yoga*' means a science that finds its material for study not in the appearances of other beings, but *in the inner world of the scientist himself*. This inner world, of course, is not worth studying — and nothing can be learned from it — if it is an impenetrable chaos. While the methods of Western science can be applied by anyone who has learned them, the scientific methods of yoga can be effectively applied only by those prepared first of all to put their own house in order through discipline and systematic inner work.

Self-knowledge, as mentioned before, is the precondition of understanding other people. It is also the precondition of understanding, at least to some extent, the inner life of beings at lower levels: animals and even plants. St Francis could communicate with animals, and so could other men and women who had attained an exceptional degree of self-mastery and self-knowledge. Reverting to our earlier way of speaking, we can say: such communicating is not possible for the computer, but only for the computer programmer. His powers certainly go far beyond those we are ordinarily familiar with and are not confined to the framework of time and space.

Ernest E. Wood, who really could speak from experience of yoga, says: 'I wish to guard the novice against the two dangers of self-judgment and the fixing of goals, and to tell him that as he is calling into expression high forces within and behind and above his present level of self he must let them do their work in him.'⁹ It is therefore neither necessary nor advisable to talk about these matters in detail. Those who are genuinely interested—not in the attainment of powers but in their own inner development—will study the lives and works of people who have put themselves under the control of 'Higher Mind' and thus broken out of our ordinary confinement of time and space. There is no lack of examples from all ages and all parts of the world.

It will serve our present purposes to have a quick look at three recent cases where the higher possibilities of the human being have manifested themselves, as it were, under our very eyes. Perhaps the first thing to be noted is that there is a conspiracy of 'official' silence about all three although they have left behind a great mass of evidence of one kind or another. The reader would search in vain if he looked for two of them in the biggest of present-day encyclopaedias, the *Encyclopaedia Britannica*; the third one receives a short mention of a highly biased kind, leaving the reader with the feeling that the case is one of hysteria and probably deliberate fraud, unworthy of serious interest.

The first case is that of Jakob Lorber, who was born in Styria, a province of Austria, in 1800. His father owned two small vineyards which produced a meagre living for the family, but he was also a musician who could play virtually all instruments and was able to earn some extra income as a conductor. His eldest son, Jakob—he had two younger brothers—learned to play the organ, piano and violin and showed exceptional musical talent but had to wait until his fortieth year before he was offered an appointment that promised to give him scope for his talents. He was on the point of leaving Graz to take up his new job at Trieste when he heard inside himself a very clear voice ordering him to 'get up, take a pen and write'. This was on March 15th, 1840, and Jakob Lorber stayed at Graz and wrote down what the inner voice dictated to him until he died, aged sixty-four, on August 24th, 1864. During these twenty-four years, he produced the equivalent of twenty-five volumes of 400 pages each, a monumental 'New Revelation'. The original manuscripts are still in existence, and they show an absolutely even flow of writing, with hardly any corrections. Many prominent men of his time were intimate friends of Lorber's; some of them supported him with food and money during the twenty-four years of his writing activity, which left hardly any time for earning a living. A few have written down their impressions of this humble and totally unpretentious man, who lived in poverty and often experienced his writing task as a very heavy burden.

The centrepiece of Lorber's writings is the *New St John's Gospel* in ten big volumes. I shall not attempt here to describe or in any way to characterise these works, all written in the first person singular—'I, Jesus Christ, am speaking.' They contain many strange things which are unacceptable to the modern mentality, but at the same time such a plethora of high wisdom and insight that it would be difficult to find anything more impressive in the whole of world literature. Lorber's books, at the same time, are full of statements on scientific matters which flatly contradicted the sciences of his time and anticipated a great deal of modern physics and astronomy. No one has ever raised the slightest doubt about the fact that the Lorber manuscripts came into existence during the years 1840–1864 and were produced by Jakob Lorber alone. There is no rational explanation for the range, profundity and precision of their contents. Lorber himself always assured, and was able to convince his friends, that none of it flowed from his own mind and that no one was more astonished at these contents than he himself.[10]

There are certain similarities between Lorber and Emanuel Swedenborg (1688–1772), who preceded him by roughly a hundred years. How is it to be explained that Swedenborg finds a place in all modern reference books and Lorber in none of them? The article on Swedenborg in the *Encyclopaedia Britannica* (15th edition) comments on his influence as follows:

Swedenborg's influence is by no means restricted to his immediate disciples. His visions and religious ideas have been a source of inspiration for a number of prominent writers, including Honoré de Balzac, Charles Baudelaire, Ralph Waldo Emerson, William Butler Yeats, and August Strindberg. His theological writings have been translated into many languages, and there is a constant flow of new editions.

Much the same could be said about Jakob Lorber. His books have been continuously in print for over a hundred years and more than a million copies have been sold. Yet his existence remains unrecognised by the 'official' organs of the modern world. This fact, and the contrast to Swedenborg, seem to me to illustrate very effectively the progressive constriction and narrowing of the modern mind. Lorber is too close to us to be tolerable; it is impossible to treat him as a legend of the distant past; yet to accept his reality and that of his 'New Revelation' and to face the implications of such an acceptance, would throw the whole apparatus of modern materialistic scientism out of gear.

The case of Edgar Cayce (1877–1945) is perhaps even more striking. He lived in the USA and left well over 14,000 stenographic records of the statements he had made during a kind of sleep, answering very specific questions from over 6,000 different people, in the course of forty-three years. These statements, generally referred to as 'readings', constitute 'one of the largest and most impressive records of psychic perception ever to emanate from a single individual. Together with their relevant records, correspondence and reports, they have been cross-indexed under thousands of subject headings and placed at the disposal of psychologists, students, writers and investigators who still come, in increasing numbers, to examine them.'[11] For the 'official' organs of the modern world, however, Edgar Cayce simply does not exist. The *Encyclopaedia Britannica* does not mention him. The chances of students of medicine, psychology, philosophy, or in fact of any other subject hearing of this great healer at their universities are almost nil.

Like Jakob Lorber, Edgar Cayce lived modestly, even in poverty, for much of his life. He certainly never exploited the immense fame he gained during his lifetime. The work his gifts imposed upon him was all too often a heavy burden on him, and, although short-tempered, he never lost his modesty and simplicity. Thousands of people asked him for medical help. Putting himself into some kind of trance, he was able to give generally accurate diagnoses of the illnesses of complete strangers living hundreds or even thousands of miles away. He said:

> Apparently I am one of the few who can lay aside their own personalities sufficiently to allow their souls to make this attunement to the universal source of knowledge — but I say this without any desire to brag about it ... I am certain all human beings have much greater powers than they are ever conscious of — if they would only be willing to pay the price of detachment from self-interest that it takes to develop those abilities. *Would you be willing, even once a year, to put aside, pass out entirely from, your own personality?*[12] [Italics are mine.]

Even more contemporary than Edgar Cayce is Therese Neumann, also known as Therese of Konnersreuth, who lived in southern Germany from 1898 to 1962. If the documentary evidence and eye-witness accounts relating to Therese Neumann cannot be accepted as reliable evidence, then *all* evidence is unreliable, nobody can ever be believed, and human knowledge is impossible. Much can be related of Therese's inner life and its extraordinary outward manifestations; but perhaps the most noteworthy fact connected with it is this: here is a sturdy, cheerful, immensely common-sensical peasant woman, who lives for thirty-five years without ingesting any liquid or any food except the daily Eucharist. This is not a legend from a remote place or time; it happened under our eyes, observed by innumerable people, investigated virtually continuously for thirty-five years, at Konnersreuth in what was called the American Zone of West Germany.

Jakob Lorber, Edgar Cayce and Therese Neumann were intensely religious personalities who never ceased to aver that all their knowledge and power came from 'Jesus Christ' — a Level infinitely above that of their own insignificance. At this suprahuman level each of them found, in their various ways, liberation from constraints that operate at the level of ordinary humanity — limits imposed by space and time, by the needs of the body and by the opacity of the computer-like mind. All three examples illustrate the paradoxical truth that such 'higher powers' cannot be acquired by any kind of attack and conquest conducted by the human personality; only when the striving for 'power' has entirely ceased and been replaced by a certain transcendental longing, often called the love of God, they may or may not be 'added unto you'.

8

The Four Fields of Knowledge

—FIELD THREE

In the face of facts such as those presented by the lives of Jakob Lorber, Edgar Cayce, Therese Neumann and indeed countless others, the modern world abandons its pragmatic attitudes, of which it is so proud, and simply shuts its eyes; for it has a methodical aversion, as I have said before, against anything pertaining to a Level of Being that is higher than that of the most humdrum and ordinary life.

This aversion is not untinged by fear. Are there not great dangers in the pursuit of self-knowledge? There are indeed, as we have already mentioned; and this takes us to a consideration of the *third field of knowledge*: the systematic study of the inner worlds of myself (field one) and of other beings (field two) *must* be balanced and complemented by an equally systematic study of *myself as an objective phenomenon*. Self-knowledge, to be healthy and complete, *must* consist of two parts—knowing my own inner world (field one) and knowing myself as I am known by others (field three). Without the latter, the former may indeed lead to the grossest and most destructive illusions.

We have direct access to field one; but no direct access to field three; as a result, our intentions tend to be much more real to us than our actions, and this can lead to a great deal of misunderstanding with other people, to whom our actions tend to be much more real than our intentions. If I derive my 'picture of myself' solely from field one, my inner experiences, I inevitably tend to see myself as 'the Centre of the Universe': everything revolves around me; when I shut my eyes the world disappears; my suffering turns the world into a vale of tears;

my happiness, into a garden of delight. A passage from the
diaries of Dr Goebbels—one of the Big Three of Hitler's
Germany—comes to mind: if we perish, he says, the whole
world will perish. But we do not need such gruesome examples.
There are harmless and mild-mannered philosophers who raise
the question of whether the tree at which they are looking will
still be there when nobody is looking. They have lost themselves in field one and have not been able to reach field three.

In field three, totally detached, objective observation is
required, unalloyed by any wishful associations. What do I
really observe? Or rather, what would I see if I could see
myself as I am seen? This is a very difficult task. Without its
accomplishment harmonious relationships with other people
are impossible; and the injunction, 'don't do to others what
you don't want them to do to you', remains meaningless if I am
unaware of my actual impact upon others.

> I once read a story of a man who died and went into the
> next world where he met a number of people some of
> whom he knew and liked and some he knew and disliked.
> But there was one person there whom he did not know and
> he could not bear him. Everything he said infuriated him
> and disgusted him—his manner, his habits, his laziness,
> his insincere way of speaking, his facial expressions—and
> it seemed to him also that he could see into this man's
> thoughts and his feelings and all his secrets and, in fact,
> into all his life. He asked the others who this impossible
> man was. They answered: 'Up here we have very special
> mirrors which are quite different from those in your
> world. This man is yourself.' Let us suppose, then, that
> you have to live with a person who is you. Perhaps this is
> what the other person has to do. Of course, if you have
> no self-observation you may actually imagine this would
> be charming and that if everyone were just like you, the
> world would indeed be a happy place. There are no limits
> to vanity and self-conceit. Now in putting yourself into
> another person's position you are also putting yourself
> into his point of view, into *how* he sees you, and hears you,
> and experiences you in your daily behaviour. You are
> seeing yourself through his eyes.[1]

This is a very vivid and accurate description of what it means to obtain knowledge in field three, and it incidentally makes it quite clear that knowledge in field one is of quite a different kind from knowledge in field three, and that the former without the latter may be worse than useless.

Everybody has a very natural curiosity with regard to what he looks like, what he sounds like and what impression he makes on others. But the 'very special mirrors' of the story do not exist on this earth, perhaps mercifully so. The shocks they would administer might be more than we could take. It is always painful to realise that there really *is* quite a lot wrong with oneself, and we possess many mechanisms to protect our-selves from this revelation. Our natural curiosity, therefore, does not take us very far into field three, and we are all too easily diverted into studying the faults of others rather than our own. Dr Nicoll reminds us of the words in the Gospels: 'Why beholdest thou the mote that is in thy brother's eye, but con-sidereth not the beam that is in thine own eye?' He points out:

> In the Greek, the word used for the mote is simply *see*. That is easy to do. But the word used for the beam in oneself is interesting. It means 'to take notice of, to detect, to acquire knowledge of, to take in a fact about, to learn, to observe, to understand'. Obviously something far more difficult is meant than merely seeing another's faults. To turn round is not easy.[2]

How, then, can we fulfil this task, so crucial for the harmony of our life with others? The methodology is set out in the books of traditional religions, albeit in a very scattered form. Perhaps the most helpful guidance in this field is to be found in the *Psychological Commentaries on the Teaching of G. I. Gurdjieff and P. D. Ouspensky* by Maurice Nicoll, from which I have already quoted several times. His guidance goes under the term of 'external considering', or putting yourself into the other person's place. This requires a very high degree of inner truthfulness and freedom. It cannot be learned in a day, and good intentions cannot succeed without protracted efforts.

What kind of effort? Nothing in this line is possible without self-awareness. To put myself into another person's situation,

I must detach myself from my own situation. Mere consciousness will not do so: it confirms me in my own situation. The computer can do nothing but produce its pre-established programme. Only the computer programmer can effect a real change, such as 'putting oneself into another person's situation'. In other words, the quality or power required is not simply consciousness—what I have called 'factor y', which enables beings to be animals—but self-awareness, 'factor z', which enables animals to be human beings. As Dr Nicoll puts it, 'External considering is very good work. It is not about whether you were right or the other person. It increases consciousness',[3] and I should add: '*to the level of self-awareness*'.

One of the things we are least aware of as regards ourselves is our own 'swing of the pendulum'. Other people notice how we contradict ourselves, but we do not. Knowledge in field three will help us to see ourselves as others see us, and therefore to see our contradictions. This is a matter of quite fundamental importance, as we shall see later. It is not as if apparent contradictions were necessarily manifestations of error; more likely, they are manifestations of Truth. Everywhere there are opposites, and we find it always difficult to keep two opposites in our mind at the same time. Others can easily observe the swing of my pendulum from one opposite to the other, just as I can easily observe the swing of theirs. But it is my task—in field three—at least to become fully aware of the swing of *my* pendulum, of the fact that *I* tend to change very often from one opinion to its opposite; and it is my task not merely to notice the change but to take note of it uncritically, i.e. without judging or justifying it. The essence of the task in field three is *uncritical self-observation*, so that we obtain cool, objective pictures of what is actually happening—not pictures *retouché* by our current opinions of right or wrong.

One of the methods of study in field three is 'taking photographs', that is, catching true glimpses of oneself, as sometimes happens when we are not aware of looking at ourselves. Dr Nicoll has this to say:

If you have taken an album of good photographs of yourself through long self-observation, then you will not have to look far in it to find in yourself what you object to so much in the other person, and then you will be able to put yourself in the other person's position, to realise that he has also this thing that you have noticed in yourself, that he has his inner difficulties, just as you have, and so on ...

The less vanity ... you have, and the more you externally consider, the less important will you think yourself.[4]

While the—necessary!—studies in field one may tend to raise one's feelings of self-importance, the counterbalancing studies in field three should lead to the realisation of one's nothingness. What am I in this great, great Universe? What am I—just one little ant among four thousand millions of them on the face of this puny little Earth! and yet, to speak with Pascal (1623–62), 'Man is only a reed, the weakest thing in nature; but he is a thinking reed'—a reed, that is to say, with self-awareness, and to that extent infinitely precious, even if, most of the time, his self-awareness remains dormant as a mere potentiality.

The main help we have in obtaining knowledge in field three comes from the fact that we are social beings; we do not live alone, but with others. And these others are a kind of mirror in which we can see ourselves as we actually are, not as we imagine ourselves to be. The best method we can follow to obtain the requisite knowledge about ourselves is therefore to observe and understand the needs, perplexities and difficulties of others, putting ourselves in their situation. One day, we may have got to the point when we can do this so perfectly that *we*, little 'egos' with our own needs, perplexities and difficulties, do not come into this picture at all: such total absence of ego would mean total objectivity and total effectiveness.

The Christian is told 'to love his neighbour as himself'. What does that mean? When a person loves himself, there is nothing standing between him who loves and him who is being loved. But when he loves his neighbour, his own little *ego* tends to stand in between. To love one's neighbour as one loves oneself, therefore, means to love without any interference from one's own ego; it means the attainment of perfect altruism, the elimination of all traces of egoism.

Just as compassion is the prerequisite of learning in the

second field of knowledge, so altruism is the prerequisite of learning in the third.

We have noted before that these two fields are not 'directly accessible' to our observation. Only through the highest moral qualities of compassion and altruism are we able to enter them.

9

The Four Fields of Knowledge

—FIELD FOUR

I

We now turn to a consideration of the *fourth field of knowledge*, the 'appearance' of the world around us. By 'appearance' I mean everything that offers itself to our senses. In the fourth field of knowledge the decisive question is always 'What do I actually observe?' and progress is attained by eliminating assumptions, notions and presuppositions as to causes, etc., that cannot be verified by sense-observation. Field four, therefore, is the real homeland of every kind of *behaviourism*: only strictly observable behaviour is of interest. All the sciences are busy in this field, and many people believe that it is the only field in which true knowledge can be obtained.

As an example, we may quote Vilfredo Pareto (1848–1923), whose *Trattato di Sociologia Generale* has been hailed as 'the greatest and noblest effort' ever undertaken in the direction of 'objective thinking without sentiment, and ... the methods by which the rational state of mind can be cultivated ... '[1] Pareto, like countless others, insists that only in what I call 'field four' can there be a 'scientific approach':

> The field in which we move is therefore the field of experience and observation strictly. We use those terms in the meanings they have in the natural sciences such as astronomy, chemistry, physiology, and so on, and not to mean those other things which it is the fashion to designate by the terms 'inner' or 'Christian' experience ... [2]

Pareto, in other words, wishes to base himself exclusively on 'experience and observation', and he restricts the meaning of these terms to facts that the outer senses, helped by instruments and other apparatus and guided by theories, can ascertain. He thereby excludes all inner experiences, like love and hate, hope and fear, joy and anguish, and even pain. This he considers the only rational approach, and a recipe for real success:

> One readily understands how the history of the sciences down to our own time is substantially a history of the battles against the methods of introspection, etymology, analysis of verbal expression ... In our day the [latter] method has been largely banished from the physical sciences, *and the advances they have made are the fruit of that proscription.* But it is still strutting about in political economy and more blatantly still in sociology; whereas if those sciences would progress, it is imperative that they should follow *the example set by the physical sciences.* [Italics are mine.][3]

Here, it is clear that Pareto is unwilling or unable to distinguish between the different Levels of Being. It is one thing to banish 'inner' knowledge from the study of inanimate nature, the lowest of the Four Levels of Being, simply because, as far as we know, there is no inner life at this level, and everything is 'appearance'. It is quite another thing to banish it from the study of human nature and behaviour at the highest of the four Levels of Being, where outer appearance is a very unimportant matter compared with inner experience.

In the second field of knowledge, the inner experience of other beings, we found that we can know most about the higher Levels and least about inanimate matter. In the fourth field of knowledge, which we are considering now, it is the other way round: we can know most about inanimate matter and least about human beings.

From Pareto's point of view, which does not recognise differences of Level of Being, 'there is not the slightest difference between the laws of political economy or sociology and the laws of the other sciences'. He can stand as a typical example of a thinker who refuses to acknowledge the hierarchy of Levels of Being and therefore cannot see any difference between a stone and a man other than a difference in 'complexity':

> The differences that do exist [lie] ... chiefly in the greater

or lesser complexity with which effects of the various laws are intertwined ...

Another difference in scientific laws lies in the possibility of isolating their effects by experiment ... Certain sciences ... can and do make extensive use of experiment. Certain others can use it but sparingly; others, such as the social sciences, little if any.[4]

With inanimate matter we can indeed experiment as we like; no amount of interference can destroy its life—for it has no life—or distort its inner experience—for there is no inner experience.

Experimentation is a valid and legitimate method of study only when it does not destroy the object under investigation. Inanimate matter cannot be destroyed; it can only be transformed. Life, consciousness and self-awareness, on the other hand, are damaged very easily and are almost invariably destroyed when the element of freedom inherent in these three powers is assumed to be non-existent.

It is not simply the complexity at the higher Levels of Being that militates against the experimental method, but, much more importantly, the fact that causality, which rules supreme at the Level of inanimate matter, is at the higher Levels put into a subservient position; it ceases to rule and is being *employed* by higher powers, for purposes unknown at the level of physics and chemistry.

When this point is missed and the attempt is made to press all sciences into the mould of physics, a certain kind of 'progress' is indeed obtained; a kind of knowledge is accumulated which, however, more likely than not becomes a barrier to understanding and even a curse from which it is hard to escape. The lower takes the place of the higher, as when the study of a great work of art confines itself to the study of the materials of which it is made.

Physics, with chemistry and astronomy, is widely considered to be the most mature of the sciences and also the most successful. The life sciences, as well as the social sciences and the so-called humanities, are thought to be less mature because they are beset by infinitely greater uncertainties. If 'maturity' were the word, we would have to say that, the more mature the object of study, the less mature is the science studying it. There is indeed more maturity in a human being than in a lump of mineral. That we have acquired more certain knowledge—of a kind—about the latter than about the former cannot surprise us if we remember that

if matter can be written m

man has to be written $m + x + y + z$.

Physics deals only with 'm', and it does so, as we have already seen, in a severely restrictive manner. Its programme of investigation can be completed, just as the study of mechanics can be said to have been completed, and this may be called 'maturity'. It is certain that the study of 'x', 'y' and 'z' can never be completed.

If we look carefully at what the various sciences in field four actually do, we find that we can divide them roughly into two groups: those that are primarily *descriptive* of what can actually be seen or otherwise experienced, and those that are primarily *instructional* of how certain systems work and can be made to produce predictable results. We might give botany as an example of the former, and chemistry of the latter. The difference between these two groups is seldom observed, with the result that most philosophies of science are found to relate only to the instructional sciences and to treat the descriptive ones as non-existing. It is not, as has often been asserted, as if the difference between 'descriptive' and 'instructional' signified merely degrees of maturity or stages in the development of a science. F. S. C. Northrop claims that 'any empirical science in its normal healthy development begins with a more purely inductive emphasis ... and then comes to maturity with deductively formulated theory *in which formal logic and mathematics play a most significant part*.'[5] This is perfectly true of 'instructional' science; Northrop chooses geometry and physics as examples, which are instructional sciences *par excellence*; but it can never be true of descriptive sciences like botany, zoology and geography, not to mention the historical sciences, whether they deal with nature or with man.

The distinction between descriptive and instructional sciences is similar to, but not identical with, that between 'sciences for understanding' and 'sciences for manipulation' which we discussed in an earlier chapter. A faithful *description* answers the question: 'What do I actually encounter?' An effective *instruction* answers a quite different question, namely: 'What must I do to obtain a certain result?' Needless to say, neither descriptive nor instructional sciences are mere accumulations of facts as presented by nature; in both cases, facts are 'purified' or 'idealised'; concepts are formed and theorems are put forward. A faithful description, however, is ruled by the concern, 'I must be careful not to leave out anything of significance', while an instruction is the more effective the more rigorously it excludes all factors that are not strictly necessary. People talk of 'Occam's razor', which is wielded to cut away everything that is superfluous from the point of view of obtaining results. We can say therefore that descriptive science is—or should be—primarily concerned with *the whole truth*; while instructional science is primarily concerned only with such *parts or aspects of truth* as are useful for manipulation. In both cases I use the word 'primarily' because this is not, and cannot be, a matter of an absolute difference.

Instructions, to be effective, must be precise, distinct, beyond doubt or dispute. It is not good enough to instruct, 'Take a small quantity of water at a temperature that is comfortably warm'. This may do for cooking but not for *exact* science. We must know precisely how much water and at precisely what temperature; there must be no room for 'subjective' interpretation. Ideally, therefore, instructional science is totally quantified, and *qualities* (such as the actual colour red, for instance) may play a part in it only when they 'correlate' with some quantitatively definable phenomenon (such as light waves of a certain frequency). Its means of advance are logic and mathematics.

In the course of this advance it has been found that there is a strange and wonderful mathematical order in physical phenomena, and this has moved the minds of some of the most thoughtful modern physicists away from the crude materialism that ruled their science in the nineteenth century, and has made them aware of a transcendent reality. Even if traditional religion, which ascribed to God 'the kingdom, the power, and the glory', remained unacceptable to them, they could not fail to recognise supreme mathematical talent somewhere in the construction and management of the Universe. Thus there is, from this side, a significant movement towards closing the infinitely harmful rift between natural science and religion. Some of the most advanced modern physicists would even agree with René Guénon's claim that 'the whole of nature amounts to no more than a symbol of transcendent realities'.[6]

If some physicists now think of God as a great mathematician, this is a significant reflection of the fact that 'instructive science' *deals only with the dead aspect of nature*. Mathematics, after all, is far removed from life. At its heights it certainly manifests a severe kind of beauty and also a captivating elegance, which may even be taken as a sign of Truth; but, equally certainly, it has no warmth, none of life's messiness of growth and decay, hope and despair, joy and suffering. This must never be overlooked or forgotten: physics and the other instructional sciences limit themselves to the lifeless aspect of reality, and this is necessarily so if the aim and purpose of science is to produce predictable results. Life, and, even more so, consciousness and self-awareness, cannot be ordered about; they have, we might say, a will of their own, which is a sign of maturity.

What we need to grasp at this point—and to inscribe on our 'map of knowledge'—is this: since physics and the other instructional sciences base themselves only on the dead aspect of nature, *they cannot lead to philosophy, if philosophy is to give us guidance on what 'life' is all about*. Nineteenth-century physics told us that life was a cosmic accident, without meaning or purpose. The best twentieth-century physicists take it all back and tell us that they deal only with specific, strictly isolated systems, showing how these systems work, or can be made to work, and that no general philosophical conclusions can (and should) ever be drawn from this knowledge.

All the same, it is evident that the instructional sciences, even though they do not lead to guidance on how to conduct our lives, are shaping our lives, through the technologies derived from them. Whether these results are for good or for evil is a question entirely outside their province. In this sense, it is correct to say that these sciences are ethically neutral. It remains true, however, that there is no science without scientists, and that questions of good and evil, even if they lie outside the province of science, cannot be considered to lie

THE FOUR FIELDS OF KNOWLEDGE—FOUR

outside the province of the scientist. It is no exaggeration today to talk about a crisis of (instructional) science. If it continues to be a juggernaut outside humanistic control there will be a reaction and revulsion against it which would not exclude the possibility of violence.

Since the instructional sciences are not concerned with the whole truth but only with those parts or aspects of truth through which *results* can be obtained, it is right that they should be judged exclusively by their results.

The claim that 'Science' brings forth 'Truth', certain, unshakeable, reliable knowledge that has been 'scientifically proved', and that this unique ability gives it a status higher than that of any other human activity—this claim on which the prestige of 'Science' is founded needs to be investigated with some care. What is proof? We may hold a great many different theories: can any of them be 'proved'? We can see right away that it is possible to 'prove' a recipe or any other instruction that takes the form of: 'If you do X, you will obtain Y.' If such an instruction does not work it is useless; if it does work, it has been 'proved'. *Pragmatism* is the philosophy that holds that the only valid idea of truth is that it *works*. The pragmatist advises: 'It is irrational to say, "When an idea is true, it works"; you should say, "When an idea works, it is true".' In its purest form, however, pragmatism has the relative sterility of a hit-and-miss method: all sorts of instructions, taken in isolation, may be found to work; but unless I have some idea of a principle or 'law' that makes a given system work my chances of extending the range of instructional knowledge are slim. The idea of proof, and therewith the idea of truth, in the instructional sciences is therefore twofold: the instruction must work, i.e. lead to predicted results, and it must also be *intelligible* in terms of established scientific principles. Phenomena that are not intelligible in this sense are of no use to instructional science and therefore of no interest. It is a methodological requirement of the instructional sciences to ignore them. Such phenomena must not be allowed to call the established scientific principles into question; there would be no pragmatic value in doing so. As I have emphasised before, the instructional sciences are not concerned with the whole truth but only with the minimum amount of truth required to make their instructions effective and reliable. It follows that proof in the instructional sciences suffers from the same limitations: It establishes that a certain set of instructions works, and that there is sufficient truth in the underlying scientific principles to allow it to work; but it does not establish that other instructions might not also work or that an entirely different set of scientific principles might not also meet the case. As is well known, the pre-Copernican instructions on how to calculate the movements inside the solar system, based on the theory that the sun moved around the earth, for a long time produced much more accurate results than the post-Copernican instructions.

What, now, is the nature of proof in the descriptive sciences? The answer is inescapable: there can be classifications, observed regularities, speculations, theorems of different grades of plausibility— *but there can never be proof*. Scientific proof can exist only in instructional science, within the limitations mentioned above, because only that can be proved which, with our minds or with our hands, we can do ourselves. Our minds can *do* geometry, mathematics and logic; we are therefore able to issue instructions that work, and thereby to establish *proof*. Equally, our hands are able to carry through a great variety of processes involving matter; we are therefore able to issue instructions on how to reach predetermined results—instructions that work—and thereby to establish proof. Without 'doing' on the basis of instructions, there can be no proof.

As far as the instructional sciences are concerned, there can be no quarrel with pragmatism; on the contrary, this is precisely where pragmatism belongs, where it has its proper place on the 'map of knowledge'. Nor can there be any quarrel with the restriction of the idea of truth to intelligible phenomena, which means disregarding unintelligible ones, and to theories of heuristic value, which means disregarding theories that prove 'infertile' and fail to lead to an extension of instructional knowledge. These are methodological requirements which, when rigorously observed, produce 'progress', i.e. the enhancement of man's competence and power in employing natural processes for his own purposes.

Endless trouble, however, arises when the methodological requirements of the instructive sciences are taken as scientific methodology *per se*. Applied to the descriptive sciences, they lead to a methodology of error. The restrictions of pragmatism, heuristic principles, or Occam's razor are not compatible with truthful description. (The importance of this point will be further emphasised when we come to consider the Doctrine of Evolutionism.)

Physics and related instructional sciences deal with inanimate matter which, as far as we know, is devoid of life, consciousness and self-awareness. At this Level of Being, there is nothing but 'outer appearance', as distinct from 'inner experience', and all we are concerned with is observable facts. Naturally, there can be nothing but facts, and when we say 'facts' we imply that they can be recognised by an observer. Unrecognised and—even more so—unrecognisable facts cannot and must not play any role in the theories of physics. It is therefore quite unproductive, at this Level, to make a distinction between '*what we can know*' and '*what actually exists*', i.e. between epistemology and ontology. When the modern physicist says: 'In our experiments we sooner or later encounter ourselves', he is merely stating the obvious, namely that the experimental results depend, not wholly but largely, on the question that the physicist has posed by means of his experimental arrangement. There is nothing mysterious about this, and it is quite wrong to conclude that it implies a disappearance of the difference between observer and observed. The Scholastic philosophers expressed this matter in a very simple way: all knowledge is obtained *per modum cognescentis*—in accordance with the cognitive powers of the knower.

The distinction between epistemology and ontology, or between '*what we can know*' and '*what actually exists*', becomes significant only as we move higher up the Chain of Being. As an example, take the phenomenon of life. We can recognise the fact of life, and this recognition has led people to assert that 'there exists in all living things an intrinsic factor—elusive, inestimable, and unmeasurable—that activates life.'[7] So they talked about 'vitalism'. But this commonsense view is not acceptable to the instructive sciences. We are told that Ernest Nagel, a philosopher of science, rang 'the death knell of vitalism' in 1951 by declaring vitalism a dead issue 'because of the infertility of vitalism as a guide in biological research and because of the superior heuristic value of alternative approaches'.[8]

The interesting and significant point is that this argument against vitalism is not concerned with its *truth* but with its *fertility*. To confuse these two is a very common error and causes a great deal of damage. A methodological principle— 'fertility'—which is perfectly legitimate as a methodological principle is substituted for the idea of truth and expanded into a philosophy with universal claims. As Karl Stern puts it, 'methods become mentalities'.[9] A statement is considered untrue not because it appears to be incompatible with experience, but because it does not serve as a guide in research and has no heuristic value; and, conversely, a theory is considered true, no matter how improbable it may be on general grounds, simply because of 'superior heuristic value'.

The task of the descriptive sciences is to describe. The practitioners of these sciences know that the world is full of marvels which make all of man's designs, theories or other productions appear as a child's fumblings. This tends to induce in many of them an attitude of scientific humility. They are not attracted to their disciplines by the Cartesian idea of making themselves 'masters and possessors of nature'.[10] A faithful description, however, must be not only accurate but also *graspable* by the human mind, and endless accumulations of facts cannot be grasped; so there is an inescapable need for classifications, generalisations, explanations—in other words, for theories that offer some suggestion as to how the facts may 'hang together'. Such theories can never be 'scientifically proved' to be true. The more comprehensive a theory is in the descriptive sciences, the more is its acceptance an act of faith.

Comprehensive theories in the descriptive sciences can be divided into two groups: those that see *intelligence or meaning* at work in what they describe, and those that see nothing but *chance and necessity*. It is obvious that neither the former nor the latter can be 'seen', i.e. sensually experienced by man. In the fourth field of knowledge there is only observation of movement and other kinds of material change; meaning or purpose, intelligence or chance, freedom or necessity, as well as life, consciousness, and self-awareness cannot be sensually observed. Only 'signs' can be found and observed; the observer has to choose the grade of significance he is willing to attribute to them. To interpret them as signs of chance and necessity is as 'unscientific' as to interpret them as signs of supra-human intelligence; the one is as much an act of faith as the other. This does not mean that all interpretations on the vertical scale, signifying grades of significance or Levels of Being, are equally true or untrue; it means simply that their truth or untruth does not rest on scientific proof but on right judgment, a power of the human mind that transcends mere logic just as the computer programmer's mind transcends that of the computer.

II

The distinctions that we are here discussing are of truly world-historical importance when we come to consider what is probably the most influential teaching of the modern age, the evolutionist doctrine. It is obvious that this doctrine cannot be classed with the instructional sciences: it belongs to the descriptive sciences. The question, therefore, is: 'What does it describe?'

'Evolution in biology', says Julian Huxley, 'is a loose and comprehensive term applied to cover any and every change occurring in the constitution of systematic units of animals and plants ... '[11] That there has been change in the constitution of species of animals and plants in the past is amply attested by the fossils found in the earth's crust; with the help of radio-active dating, they have been put into historical sequence with a very high degree of scientific certainty. Evolution, as a generalisation within the descriptive science of biological change, can for this and also for other reasons be taken as established beyond any doubt whatever.

The evolutionist doctrine, however, is a very different matter. It is not content to confine itself to a systematic description of biological change but purports to prove and explain it in much the same manner as proof and explanation is offered in the instructional sciences. This is a philosophical error of the most disastrous consequences.

'Darwin', we are told, 'did two things: he showed that evolution was in fact contradicting scriptural legends of creation and that its cause, natural selection, was automatic with no room for divine guidance or design.'[12] It should be obvious to anyone capable of philosophical thinking that scientific observation as such can never do these 'two things'. 'Creation', 'divine guidance' and 'divine design' are completely outside scientific observation, and so would be their absence. Every animal or plant breeder knows beyond doubt that selection, including 'natural selection', produces change; it is therefore scientifically correct to say that 'natural selection has been *proved* to be an agent of evolutionary change'—we can, in fact, prove it by doing. But it is totally illegitimate to claim that the discovery of this mechanism—natural selection—proves that the cause of evolution 'was automatic with no room for divine guidance or design'. It can be proved that people get money by finding it in the street; but no one would consider this sufficient reason for the assumption that all incomes are earned in this way.

The Doctrine of Evolutionism is generally presented in a manner that betrays, and offends against, all principles of scientific probity. It starts with the explanation of changes in living beings; but without warning, as it were, it suddenly purports to explain not only the development of consciousness, self-awareness, language and social institutions but also the origin of life itself. Imagination and speculation run riot; anything will do to explain everything. 'Evolution', we are told, 'is accepted by all biologists and natural selection is recognised as its cause ... ' As the origin of life is described as a 'major step in evolution',[13] we are asked to believe that inanimate matter is a masterful practitioner of natural selection. For the Doctrine of Evolutionism, any possibility, no matter how remote, is perfectly acceptable as scientific proof that the thing actually happened:

> When a sample atmosphere of hydrogen, water vapour, ammonia, and methane was subjected to electric discharges and ultra-violet light, large numbers of organic compounds ... were obtained by automatic synthesis. This proved that a pre-biological synthesis of complex compounds was possible.[14]

On this basis we are expected to believe that living beings

suddenly made their appearance by pure chance and, having made their appearance, were able to maintain themselves in the general chaos:

> It is not unreasonable to suppose that life originated in a watery 'soup' of pre-biological organic compounds and that living organisms arose later by surrounding quantities of these compounds by membranes that made them into 'cells'. This is usually considered the starting point of organic ('Darwinian') evolution.[15]

One can just see it, can't one—organic compounds getting together and surrounding themselves by membranes (nothing could be simpler for these clever compounds), and lo! there is the cell, and once the cell has been born there is nothing to stop the emergence of Shakespeare, although it will obviously take a bit of time. There is therefore no need to speak of miracles—or to admit any lack of knowledge. It is one of the great paradoxes of our age that people claiming the proud title of 'scientist' dare to offer such undisciplined and reckless speculations as contributions to scientific knowledge—and that they get away with it!

The late Dr Karl Stern, a psychiatrist with great insight, has commented thus:

> If we present, for the sake of argument, the theory of evolution in a most scientific formulation, we have to say something like this: 'At a certain moment of time the temperature of the Earth was such that it became most favourable for the aggregation of carbon atoms and oxygen with the nitrogen–hydrogen combination, and that from random occurrences of large clusters molecules occurred which were most favourably structured for the coming about of life, and from that point it went on through vast stretches of time, until through processes of natural selection a being finally occurred which is capable of choosing love over hate and justice over injustice, of writing poetry like that of Dante, composing music like that of Mozart, and making drawings like those of Leonardo. Of course, such a view of cosmogenesis is crazy. And I do not at all mean crazy in the sense of slangy

invective but rather in the technical meaning of psychotic. Indeed such a view has much in common with certain aspects of schizophrenic thinking.[16]

The fact remains, however, that this kind of thinking is being offered as objective science not only to biologists but to everybody eager to find out the truth about the origin, meaning and purpose of human existence on Earth, and in particular that, all over the world, virtually all children are subjected to indoctrination along the lines described.[17]

It is the task of science to observe and to report on its observations. It is not useful for it to postulate the existence of causative agents, like 'Creator', 'intelligences' or 'designers', who are outside all possibilities of direct observations. 'Let us see how far we can explain phenomena by observable causes' is an eminently sensible and, in fact, very fruitful methodological principle. Evolutionism, however, turns methodology into a faith that excludes, *ex hypothesi*, the possibility of all higher grades of significance. The whole of nature, which obviously includes mankind, is taken as the product of chance and necessity *and nothing else*; there is neither meaning, nor purpose, nor intelligence in it — 'a tale told by an idiot, signifying nothing'. This is The Faith, and all contradicting observations have to be either ignored or interpreted in such a way that The Faith is upheld.

Evolutionism as currently presented has no basis in science. It can be described as a peculiarly degraded religion, many of whose high priests do not even believe in what they proclaim. Despite widespread disbelief, the doctrinaire propaganda which insists that scientific knowledge of evolution leaves no room for any higher faith continues unabated. Counter-arguments are simply ignored. The article on 'Evolution' in *The New Encyclopaedia Britannica* (1975) finishes with a section entitled 'The acceptance of evolution', claiming that 'objections to evolution have come from theological and, for a time, from political standpoints.'[18] Who would suspect, when reading this, that the most serious objections have been raised by numerous biologists and other scientists of unimpeachable credentials? It is evidently thought unwise to mention them, and books such as Douglas Dewar's *The Transformist Illusion*,[19] which offers an overwhelming refutation of evolutionism on purely scientific grounds, are not considered fit for inclusion in the bibliography on the subject. Evolutionism is not science; it is science fiction, even a kind of hoax. It is a hoax that has succeeded too well and has imprisoned modern man in what looks like an irreconcilable conflict between 'science' and 'religion'. It has destroyed all faiths that pull mankind up and has substituted a faith that pulls mankind down. *Nil admirari.* Chance and necessity and the utilitarian mechanism of natural selection may produce curiosities, improbabilities and atrocities, but nothing that can be *admired* as an achievement—just as winning a prize in a lottery cannot elicit admiration. There is nothing 'higher' and nothing 'lower'; everything is much of a muchness, even though some things are more complex than others—just by chance. Evolutionism, purporting to explain all and everything solely and exclusively by natural selection for adaptation and survival, is the most extreme product of the materialistic utilitarianism of the nineteenth century. The inability of twentieth-century thought to rid itself of this imposture is a failure that may well cause the collapse of Western civilisation. For it is impossible for any civilisation to survive without a faith in meanings and values transcending the utilitarianism of comfort and survival—in other words, without a religious faith. Martin Lings observes:

There can be little doubt that in the modern world more cases of loss of religious faith are to be traced to the theory of evolution as their immediate cause than to anything else. It is true, surprising as it may seem, that many people still contrive to live out their lives in a tepid and precarious combination of religion and evolutionism. But for the more logically minded, there is no option but to choose between the two, that is, between the doctrine of the fall of man and the 'doctrine' of the rise of man, and to reject altogether the one not chosen ...

Millions of our contemporaries have chosen evolutionism on the grounds that evolution is a 'scientifically proved truth', as many of them were taught it at school; the gulf between them and religion is widened still further by the fact that the religious man, unless he happens to be a scientist, is unable to make a bridge between himself and them by producing the right *initial* argument, which must be on the scientific plane.[20]

If it is not on the 'scientific plane', he will be shouted down 'and reduced to silence by all sorts of scientific jargon'. The truth of the matter, however, is that the initial argument must *not* be on the scientific plane; it must be *philosophical*. It amounts simply to this: descriptive science becomes unscientific and illegitimate when it indulges in comprehensive explanatory theories which can be neither verified nor falsified by experiment. Such theories are not 'science' but 'faith'.

III

What we can say at this stage of our exposition is that there is no possibility of deriving a *valid* faith from the study of the fourth field of knowledge alone, which offers nothing but *observations of appearances*.

All the same, it can be shown that the ever more precise, meticulous, conscientious and imaginative observation of appearances, such as the best of modern scientists engage in, produces increasing amounts of evidence that totally belie the materialistic utilitarianism of the nineteenth century. This is not the place for a detailed exposition of these findings. I can only mention again the conclusions reached by the late Dr Wilder Penfield, which are supported, in a most interesting way, by the researches of Professor Harold Saxton Burr, professor of anatomy (now *emeritus*), Yale University School of Medicine. His 'adventure in science' began in 1935 and continued for forty years: a search for the mysterious factor which organises inanimate material into living beings and then maintains them. The molecules and cells of the human body are constantly disintegrated and rebuilt from new material.

All protein in the body, for example, is 'turned over' every six months and in some organs such as the liver, the protein is renewed more frequently. When we meet a friend we have not seen for six months there is not one molecule in his face which was there when we last saw him.[21]

Professor Burr and his collaborators discovered

> *that man—and, in fact, all forms—are ordered and controlled by*
> *electrodynamic fields which can be measured and mapped with*
> *precision ...*

Though almost inconceivably complicated, the 'fields of life' are of the same nature as the simpler fields known to modern physics and obedient to the same laws. Like the fields of physics, they are part of the organisation of the Universe and are influenced by the vast forces of space. Like the fields of physics, too, they have organising and directing qualities which have been revealed by many thousands of experiments.

Organisation and direction, the direct opposite of chance, imply purpose. So the fields of life offer purely electronic, instrumental evidence that man is no accident. On the contrary, he is an integral part of the Cosmos, embedded in its all-powerful fields, subject to its inflexible laws and a participant in the destiny and purpose of the Universe.[22]

The idea that the marvels of living nature are nothing but complex chemistry, evolved through natural selection, is thereby effectively destroyed, although the organising power of *fields* remains a total mystery. Professor Burr's dethronement of chemistry and therewith also of biochemistry, with all its DNA-mythology of molecules becoming information systems, is certainly a very big step in the right direction. 'To be sure,' says Professor Burr,

chemistry is of great importance, because this is the gasoline that makes the buggy go, but the chemistry of a living system does not determine the functional properties of a living system any more than changing the gas makes a Rolls-Royce out of a Ford. The chemistry provides the energy, but the electrical phenomena of the electro-dynamic field determine the direction in which energy flows within the living system. Therefore they are of prime importance in understanding the growth and development of all living things.[23]

It is highly significant that, as observational science becomes more refined and accurate, the rash utilitarian–materialistic doctrines of the nineteenth century are crumbling away one by one, in spite of the fact that most scientists insist on limiting their work to the fourth field of knowledge, whereby, as we have shown before, they methodically exclude all evidence of forces deriving from the higher Levels of Being and confine themselves to the dead aspect of the Universe. This methodical self-limitation makes sense—very good sense—for the instructional sciences, if only because the higher powers, life, consciousness and self-awareness, are beyond 'instruction': they *do* the instructing! But it makes no sense at all for the descriptive sciences: what is the value of a description if it omits the most interesting aspects and features of the object to be described? Happily, there are now quite a number of scientists, like the zoologist Adolf Portmann and the botanist Heinrich Zoller (to name the two from whom I have benefited the most), both at Basle University, who have had the courage to break out of the prison walls built by the modern Cartesians and to show us the kingdom and the power and the glory of a mysteriously meaningful Universe.

To do so is the function of the descriptive sciences. If it were not, why bother with them? The modern Cartesians, bent on making themselves the 'masters and possessors of nature', may answer, with F. S. C. Northrop, that description is of value only if it leads to action, i.e. to an instruction as to how to obtain results, and that the descriptive sciences are therefore nothing but instructional sciences in their early stage of immaturity. If this line of argument were fully accepted—as it has increasingly tended to be since Descartes—the scientific picture of the world would necessarily be one of desolation and abomination, and civilisation would become the same: it would die.

IV

The four fields of knowledge can be clearly distinguished; knowledge itself is nevertheless a unity. The main purpose of showing the four fields separately is to make the unity appear in its plenitude. A few examples may be given of what this analysis helps us to understand.

(1) The unity of knowledge is destroyed when one or several of the four fields of knowledge remain uncultivated, and also when cultivations take place in one field with instruments and methodologies that are appropriate only in quite another field.

(2) To obtain clarity, it is necessary to relate the four fields of knowledge to the four Levels of Being. We have already touched on this in passing—that, for instance, but little can be learned about human nature by anyone who confines his studies to the fourth field of knowledge, the field of appearances. Similarly, little if anything can normally be learned about the mineral kingdom from studies of one's own inner experiences, unless certain higher sensitivities have been developed as in the cases of people like Lorber, Cayce and Therese Neumann, among many others.

(3) The instructional sciences do well to confine their attention exclusively to field four, since only in this field of appearances can mathematical precision be obtained; the descriptive sciences, on the other hand, betray their calling when they ape the instructional sciences and confine themselves to the observation of appearances. If they cannot penetrate to *meaning* and *purpose*, i.e. ideas derivable only from inner experience (fields one and two), they remain sterile and almost useless for humanity—except that they may be useful as producers of 'inventories', which hardly deserves the noble name of science.

(4) Self-knowledge, so universally praised as the most valuable, remains worse than useless if based solely on a study of field one, one's own inner experiences; it *must* be balanced by an equally intensive study of field three, so that we learn to know ourselves as others know us. This point is all too often overlooked, because of a failure to distinguish between field one and field three.

(5) Finally, social knowledge, that is the knowledge needed for the establishment of harmonious relationships between people: we have no direct access to field two—the inner experiences of other beings. To obtain indirect access is one of the most important tasks of man, seen as a social being. This indirect access can be obtained only through self-knowledge, which shows that it is a grave error to blame a man who

pursues self-knowledge for 'turning his back on society'. The opposite would be more nearly true: that a man who fails to pursue self-knowledge is and remains a danger to society, for he will tend to misunderstand everything that other people say or do and remain blissfully unaware of many of the things he does himself.

10

Two Types of Problem

I

First, we dealt with 'the World'—its four Levels of Being; second, with 'Man'—his equipment wherewith to meet the world: to what extent is it adequate for this encounter? And then, third, we dealt with learning about the world and about oneself—the four fields of knowledge. It remains for us to look at what it means to live in this world.

To live means to *cope*, to contend and keep level with all sorts of circumstances, many of them difficult. Difficult circumstances present problems, and it might be said that living means, above all else, dealing with problems.

Unsolved problems tend to cause a kind of existential anguish. Whether this has always been so may well be questioned, but it is certainly so in the modern world, and part of the modern battle against anguish is the Cartesian approach: 'Deal only with ideas that are distinct, precise and certain beyond any reasonable doubt; therefore: rely on geometry, mathematics, quantification, measurement and exact observation.' This is the way, the only way (we are told) to solve problems; this is the road, the only road, of progress; if only we abandon all sentiment and other irrationalities, all problems can and will be solved. We live in the age of the Reign of Quantity—which, incidentally, is the title of a difficult and important book[1] by René Guénon, one of the few significant metaphysicians of our time. Quantification and cost—benefit analysis are said to be the answer to most, if not all, of our problems, although where we are dealing with somewhat complex beings, like humans, or complex systems, like societies, it may still take a little time for sufficient data to be assembled and analysed. Our civilisation is uniquely expert in problem-solving, and there are more scientists and similar people in the world today than there have been in all previous generations added together—and they are not wasting their time contemplating the marvels of the Universe or trying to acquire self-knowledge: they are *solving problems*. (I could imagine someone becoming slightly anxious at this point and inquiring: 'If this is so, aren't we running out of problems?' But it would be easy to reassure him: we have more and bigger problems now than any previous generation could boast, even problems of survival.)

This extraordinary situation might lead us to inquire into the nature of 'problems'. We know there are solved problems and unsolved problems. The former, we may feel, do not present a problem; but as regards the latter: are there problems that are not merely unsolved but insoluble?

First, let us look at solved problems. Take a design problem— say, how to make a two-wheeled, man-powered means of transportation. Various solutions are offered, which gradually and increasingly converge until, finally, a design emerges which is simply 'the answer'—a bicycle, an answer that turns out to be amazingly stable in time. Why is this answer so stable? Simply because it complies with the laws of the Universe—laws at the level of inanimate nature.

I propose to call problems of this nature *convergent problems*. The more intelligently you study them, the more—whoever you are—the answers converge. They may be classified into 'convergent problem solved' and 'convergent problem as yet unsolved'. The words 'as yet' are important; for there is no reason, in principle, why they should not be solved some day. Everything takes time, and there simply has not yet been time enough to get around to solving them. What is needed is more time, more money for research and development (R&D) and, maybe, more talent.

It also happens, however, that a number of highly able people set out to study a problem and come up with answers that contradict one another. They do not converge. On the contrary, the more they are clarified and logically developed, the more they *diverge*, until some of them appear to be the exact opposites of the others. For example, life presents us with a very big problem—not the technical problem of two-wheeled transport, but the human problem of how to educate our children. We cannot escape it; we have to face it, and we ask a number of equally intelligent people to advise us. Some of them, on the basis of a very clear intuition, tell us this: Education is the process by which existing culture is passed on to the next generation. Those who have (or are supposed to have) knowledge and experience *teach*, and those who as yet lack knowledge and experience *learn*. This is quite clear, and implies that there must be a situation of authority and discipline.

Nothing could be simpler, truer, more logical and straightforward. When it is a matter of passing on existing knowledge from the knowers to the learners, there must be discipline among the learners to receive what is being offered. In other words, education calls for the establishment of authority for the teachers and for discipline and obedience on the part of the pupils.

Now, another group of our advisers, having gone into the problem with the utmost care, says this: 'Education is nothing more or less than the provision of a *facility*. The educator is like a good gardener, who is concerned to make available good, healthy, fertile soil in which a young plant can grow strong roots and then extract the nutrients it requires. The young plant will develop in accordance with its own laws of being, which are far more subtle than any human being can fathom, and will develop best when it has the greatest possible freedom to choose exactly the nutrients it needs.' Education, in other words, as seen by this second group, calls for the establishment not of discipline and obedience, but of freedom—the greatest possible freedom.

If our first group of advisers is right, discipline and obedience are 'a good thing', and it can be argued with perfect logic that if something is 'a good thing', more of it will be an even better thing; and this line of logic leads to the conclusion that perfect discipline and obedience would be a perfect thing ... and the school would become a prison.

Our second group of advisers, on the other hand, argues that in education freedom is 'a good thing'. If so, more freedom will be an even better thing, and perfect freedom would produce perfect education. The school would become a wilderness, even a kind of lunatic asylum.

Freedom and discipline/obedience—here is a perfect pair of opposites. No compromise is possible. It is either the one or the other, in any real situation. It is either 'Do as you like' or 'Do as I tell you'.

Logic does not help us because it insists that if a thing is true, its opposite cannot be true at the same time. It also insists that, if a thing is good, more of it will be better. Here, however, we have a very typical and very basic problem, which I call a *divergent problem*, and it does not yield to ordinary, 'straight-line' logic; it demonstrates that life is bigger than logic.

'What is the best method of education?' in short presents a divergent problem *par excellence*. The answers tend to diverge; the more logical and consistent they are, the greater is the divergence. There is 'freedom' versus 'discipline and obedience'. There is no solution—and yet, some educators are better than others. How do they do it? One way to find out is to ask them. If we explained to them our philosophical difficulties they might show signs of irritation with this intellectual approach. 'Look here,' they might say, 'all this is far too clever for me. The point is: You must *love* the little horrors.' Love, empathy, *participation mystique*, understanding, compassion—these are faculties of a higher order than those required for the implementation of any policy of discipline or of freedom. To mobilise these higher faculties or forces, to have them available not simply as occasional impulses but permanently: that requires a high level of self-awareness, and that makes a great educator.

Education presents the classical example of a divergent problem, and so of course does politics, where the most frequently encountered pair of opposites is 'freedom' and 'equality', which in fact means freedom *versus* equality, equality *versus* freedom. For if matters are left free, i.e. left to themselves, the strong will prosper and the weak will suffer, and there will be no trace of equality. The enforcement of equality, on the other hand, requires the curtailment of freedom—*unless something intervenes from a higher level*. I do not know who coined the slogan of the French Revolution;* he must

* Some people say it was Louis-Claude de Saint Martin (1743–1803) who signed his works *Le Philosophe inconnu*, the Unknown Philosopher.

have been a person of rare insight. To the pair of opposites, *liberté* versus *egalité*, irreconcilable in ordinary logic, he added a third factor or force—*fraternité*, brotherliness—which comes from a higher level. How do we recognise it as coming from a higher level than *liberté* or *egalité*? These can be instituted by legislative action backed by force, but *fraternité* is a human quality beyond the reach of institutions, beyond the level of manipulation. It can be achieved, and indeed is often being achieved, but only by individual persons mobilising their own higher forces and faculties, in short, becoming better people. 'How do you make people become better?' This question is constantly being asked, and it merely shows that the essential point has been missed altogether. The idea of *making* people better belongs to the level of manipulation, the same level at which the opposites exist and at which their reconciliation is impossible.

The moment we recognise that there are two different types of problems with which we have to deal on our journey through life—'convergent' and 'divergent' problems—some very interesting questions arise in our minds, such as:

How can I recognise whether a problem belongs to the one type or the other?
What is it that constitutes the difference?
What is it that constitutes the solution of a problem in each of the two types?
Is there 'progress'? Can solutions be accumulated?

The attempt to deal with questions of this kind will undoubtedly lead to many further explorations.

Let us begin then with the question of recognition. With a convergent problem, as already mentioned, the answers suggested for its solution tend to converge, to become increasingly precise; they can be finalised and written down in the form of an instruction. Once the answer has been found, the problem ceases to be interesting: a solved problem is a dead problem. To make use of the solution does not require any higher faculties or abilities—the challenge is gone, the work is done. Whoever makes use of the solution can remain relatively passive; he is a recipient, getting something for nothing, as it were. Convergent problems relate to the dead aspect of the Universe, where manipulation can proceed without let or hindrance and where man can make himself 'master and possessor', because the subtle, higher forces, which we have labelled life, consciousness and self-awareness, are not there to complicate matters. Wherever these higher forces intervene to a significant extent, the problem ceases to be convergent. We can say, therefore, that *convergence* may be expected with regard to any problem that does not involve life, consciousness or self-awareness, which means in the fields of physics, chemistry, astronomy, in abstract subjects like geometry and mathematics, or in games like chess.

The moment we are dealing with problems involving the higher Levels of Being, we must expect *divergence*, for there enters, to however modest a degree, the element of freedom and inner experience. Looked at from another angle, we see the most universal pair of opposites, the very hallmark of life: growth and decay. Growth thrives on freedom (I mean healthy growth—pathological growth is really a form of decay), while the forces of decay and dissolution can be contained only through some kind of order. These basic pairs of opposites—

Growth *versus* Decay

and Freedom *versus* Order—

are encountered wherever there is life, consciousness, self-awareness. As we have seen, it is pairs of opposites that make a problem divergent, while the absence of pairs of opposites (of this basic character) ensures convergence.

The methodology of problem-solving, as can easily be observed, is what we might call 'the laboratory approach'. It consists of eliminating all factors that cannot be strictly controlled or, at least, accurately measured and 'allowed for'. What remains is no longer a part of real life with all its unpredictabilities, but an isolated system posing convergent, and therefore in principle *soluble*, problems. The solution of a convergent problem, at the same time, proves something about the isolated system, but nothing at all about matters outside and beyond it.

I have said that to solve a problem is to kill it. There is nothing wrong with 'killing' a convergent problem, for it relates to what remains after life, consciousness and self-awareness have already been eliminated. But can—or should—divergent problems be killed? (The words 'final solution' still have a terrible ring in the ears of my generation.)

Divergent problems cannot be killed; they cannot be solved in the sense of establishing the 'correct formula'. They can however be transcended. A pair of opposites—like freedom and order—are opposites at the level of ordinary life, but they cease to be opposites at the higher level, the really *human* level, where self-awareness plays its proper role. It is then that such higher forces as love and compassion, understanding and empathy, become available, not simply as occasional impulses (which they are at the lower level) but as a regular and reliable resource. Opposites cease to be opposites; they lie down together peacefully like the lion and the lamb in the study of Saint Hieronymus (who on Dürer's famous picture represents 'the higher level').

How can opposites cease to be opposites when a 'higher force' is present? How is it that liberty and equality cease to be mutually antagonistic and become 'reconciled' when brotherliness is present? These are not logical but *existential* questions. The main concern of existentialism, it has been noted,[2] is that experience has to be admitted as evidence, which implies that without experience there is no evidence. That opposites are transcended when 'higher forces'—like love and compassion— intervene is not a matter to be argued in terms of logic: it has to be experienced in one's actual existence (hence: 'existentialism'). Here is a family, let us say, with two big boys and two small girls; freedom prevails, and it does not destroy equality because brotherliness controls the use of the superior power possessed by the big boys.

It is important for us to become fully aware of these pairs of opposites. Our logical mind does not like them: it generally operates on the either–or or yes–no principle, like a computer. So, at any one time it wishes to give its exclusive allegiance to either the one or the other of the pair, and as this exclusiveness inevitably leads to an ever more obvious loss of realism and truth, the mind suddenly changes sides, often without even noticing it. It swings like a pendulum from one opposite to the other, and every time there is a feeling of 'making up one's mind afresh'; or else the mind becomes rigid and lifeless, fixing itself on one side of the pair of opposites and feeling that now 'the problem has been solved'.

The pairs of opposites, of which freedom and order and growth and decay are the most basic, put tension into the world, a tension that sharpens man's sensitivity and increases his self-awareness. No real understanding is possible without awareness of these pairs of opposites, which, as it were, permeate everything man does.

In the life of societies there is the need for justice and also the need for mercy. 'Justice without mercy', said Thomas Aquinas, 'is cruelty; mercy without justice is the mother of dissolution'[3]—a very clear identification of a divergent problem. Justice is a denial of mercy, and mercy is a denial of justice. Only a higher force—wisdom—can reconcile these opposites. The problem cannot be solved; but wisdom can transcend it. Similarly, societies need stability *and* change, tradition *and* innovation; public interest *and* private interest; planning *and* *laissez-faire*; order *and* freedom; growth *and* decay: everywhere society's health depends on the simultaneous pursuit of mutually opposed activities or aims. The adoption of a final solution means a kind of death sentence for man's humanity and spells either cruelty or dissolution, or generally both.

Divergent problems offend the logical mind which wishes to remove tension by coming down on one side or the other; but they provoke, stimulate and sharpen the higher human faculties without which man is nothing but a clever animal. A refusal to accept the divergency of divergent problems causes these higher faculties to remain dormant and to wither away, and when this happens the 'clever animal' is more likely than not to destroy itself.

Man's life can thus be seen and understood as a succession of divergent problems which are inevitably encountered and have to be coped with in some way. They are refractory to mere logic and discursive reason, and constitute, as it were, a strain-and-stretch apparatus to develop the Whole Man, and that means to develop man's supra-logical faculties. All traditional cultures have seen life as a school and have recognised, in one way or another, the essentiality of this teaching force.

II

At this point, it may be appropriate to say a few words about art. Today, as far as art is concerned, there seems to be nothing at all to go by and anything will do. Who dares to say 'boo' to anything claiming to be 'art ahead of its time'? However, we need not be so timid. We can obtain reliable bearings by relating art to the human being, which consists, as it were, of feeling, thinking and willing. If art aims primarily to affect our feelings we may call it entertainment; if it aims primarily to affect our will we may call it propaganda. These two, entertainment and propaganda, we can recognise as a pair of opposites, and we have no difficulty is sensing that something is missing. No great artist has ever turned his back on either entertainment or propaganda, or was ever satisfied with just these two. Invariably he strove to communicate truth, the *power* of truth, by appealing to man's higher intellectual faculties, which are supra-rational. Entertainment and propaganda by themselves do not give us power but exert power over us. When they are transcended by, and made subservient to, the communication of Truth, art helps us to develop our higher faculties, and this is all that matters. If art is to have any real value, says Ananda K. Coomaraswamy,

> if it is to nourish and make the best part of us grow, as plants are nourished and grow in suitable soils, it is to the understanding and not to fine feelings that an appeal must be made. In one respect the public is right; it always wants to know what a work of art is 'about' ... Let us tell them the painful truth that most of these (great) works of art are about God, whom we never mention in polite society. Let us admit that if we are to offer an education in agreement with the innermost nature and eloquence of [these great works of art] themselves, that this will not be an education in sensibility, but an education in philosophy, in Plato's and Aristotle's sense of the word, for whom *it means ontology and theology and the map of life, and a wisdom to be applied to everyday matters.*[4] [My italics added.]

All great works of art are 'about God' in the sense of showing to the perplexed human being the path, the way up the mountain, providing a guide for the perplexed. We may again remind ourselves of one of the greatest examples of such art, Dante's *Divine Comedy*.[5] Dante wrote to be read by ordinary men and women, not by people with sufficient private means to be mainly interested in fine feelings. 'The whole work', he explains, 'was undertaken not for a speculative but a practical end ... the purpose of the whole is to remove those living in this life from a state of misery, and lead them into a state of felicity.'[6] The pilgrim—Dante himself—*nel mezzo del cammin di nostra vita*, that is, at the height of his powers and outward success, suddenly realises that he is not at the height at all but, on the contrary, 'in a dark wood, where the right way was lost'.

> Ah! how hard a thing it is to tell
> what this wild and rough and difficult wood was,
> which in thought renews my fear!
> So bitter that death is little more.

He cannot remember how he ever got there,

> so full was I of slumber at that moment
> when I abandoned the true way.

Having 'found himself', Dante looks up and sees the mountain,

> clothed already with the rays of the planet [the sun]
> which leads man aright along every path,

the very mountain he had meant to climb. He makes a new attempt; but he finds his way barred by three animals: first

> at the beginning of the steep
> [by] a she-leopard, light and very nimble,
> which was covered with a spotted coat.
> And she did not withdraw from before my face,
> nay, hindered so my road *that I often turned to go back*.

Light, very nimble, with a spotted coat—all the pleasant temptations of life, to which he had got used to yielding. There is worse to come—a lion, fearful in his pride, and a she-wolf

> which in her leanness seemed laden with all cravings,
> and ere now had made many folk to live forlorn,—
> she brought on me so much heaviness,
> with the fear that came from sight of her,
> *that I lost hope ...*

Dante, however is seen 'from heaven' by Beatrice, who wants to help him. She cannot do so herself, as he has sunk too low for religion to reach him, and so she asks Art, in the person of Virgil, to guide him out of 'this savage place'. True art is the intermediary between man's ordinary nature and his higher potentialities, and so Dante accepts Virgil:

> Thou by thy words has so disposed my heart
> with desire of going,
> that I have returned to my first intent.
> Now go, for one sole will is in us both:
> thou leader, thou lord, and thou master.

Only the truth can be accepted as leader, lord and master. To treasure art simply for its beauty is to miss the point. The true function of art is 'so to dispose the heart with desire of going' 'up the mountain', *which is what we really wish to do but keep forgetting*, that we 'return to our first intent'.

The whole of great literature deals with divergent problems. To read such literature — even the Bible — simply 'as literature', as if its main purpose were poetry, imagination, artistic expression with a specially apt use of words and similes, is to turn the sublime into the trivial.

III

Many people today call for a new moral basis of society, a new foundation of ethics. When they say 'new', they seem to forget that they are dealing with divergent problems, which do not call for new inventions but for the development of man's higher faculties and their application. 'Some rise by sin and some by virtue fall,' says Shakespeare in *Measure for Measure*, insisting that it is not good enough to decide that virtue is good and vice is bad (which they are!); that the important thing is whether a person rises to his higher potentialities or falls away from them. Normally, men rise through virtue; but if virtue is merely external and lacks inner power, it merely makes them complacent and they fail to develop; similarly, what by ordinary standards is sin may set in motion the all-important process of development, if its shock causes a man to awake his higher faculties which had previously been asleep. To quote an example from the Eastern traditions, 'By what men fall by that they rise,' says the Kular nava Tantra. All traditional wisdom, of which both Dante and Shakespeare are outstanding representatives, transcends ordinary, calculating logic and defines 'The Good' as that which helps us to become truly human by developing our higher faculties—which are conditional on, and also part of, self-awareness. Without them, there is no humanity, as distinct from the animal kingdom, and the question of what is 'The Good' reduces itself to Darwinian questions of adaptation and survival and the utilitarianism of 'the greatest happiness of the greatest number', where happiness rarely implies anything more than comfort and excitement.

In fact, however, people do not accept these 'reductions'. Even when, being well adapted, they survive with plenty of comfort and excitement, they go on asking—'What is "Good"? What is "Goodness"? What is "Evil"? What is "Sin"? What must I do to live a worth-while life?'

In the whole of philosophy, there is no subject in greater disarray than ethics. Anyone asking for the bread of guidance on how to conduct himself, and turning to the professors of ethics, will not even receive a stone but just a torrent of 'opinions'. With very few exceptions, they embark upon an investigation into ethics without any prior clarification of the purpose of human life on Earth. It is obviously impossible to decide what is good or bad, right or wrong, virtuous or evil, without an idea of purpose: good for what?, etc. To ask the question of purpose has been called 'the naturalistic fallacy'— virtue is its own reward! None of the great teachers of mankind would have been satisfied with such an evasion. If a thing is said to be good but no one can tell me what it is good *for*, how could I be expected to take any interest in it? If our guide, our annotated Map of Life, cannot show us where The Good is situated and how it can be reached, it is worthless.

Let us recapitulate. The first Great Truth we have discussed is the hierarchic structure of the World—at least four great Levels of Being, with new powers added on the upward path. At the human level, we can clearly perceive that it is open-ended. There is no discernible limit to what man can do; he seems to be *capax universi*, as the ancients used to say, and what *one* person has done henceforth shines like a light in darkness as a capability of man, even if no second person is ever found able to do it again. The human being, even in full maturity, is obviously not a finished product, although some are undoubtedly more 'finished' than others. With most people, the specifically human faculty of self-awareness remains until the end of their lives only a germ of a faculty, so under-developed that it rarely becomes active, and then only for short moments at a time. This is precisely the 'talent' that, according to traditional teachings, we can and should develop threefold, even tenfold, and which we should on no account bury in the ground for safekeeping.

We have been able to touch only lightly on the various 'progressions' we notice when contemplating the four Levels of Being, from the lifeless mineral to the self-aware person and onward to the most perfect, most thoroughly integrated, enlightened, free 'person' we can conceive. Through these extrapolations it is possible for us not only to obtain a clear understanding of what our ancestors were concerned with when they talked about God but also to recognise the one and only direction of development that would give sense and meaning to our life on Earth.

The second Great Truth is that of *adaequatio*—that every-thing in the world around us must be matched, as it were, with some sense, faculty or power within us; otherwise we remain unaware of its existence. There is, therefore, a hierarchic structure of gifts inside us; and, not surprisingly, the higher the gift the more rarely is it to be found in a highly developed form, and the greater are the efforts required for its development. To enhance our Level of Being we have to adopt a life-style conducive to such enhancement, which means one that grants our lower nature just the attention and care it requires and leaves us with plenty of time and free attention for the pursuit of our higher development.

A central part of this pursuit is the cultivation of the four fields of knowledge. The quality of our understanding depends decisively on the detachment, objectivity and care with which we learn to study ourselves—both what goes on inside us (field one) and what we are as objective phenomena in the eyes of others (field three). Instruction on how to cultivate self-knowledge of this dual kind is the main content of all traditional religious teachings but has been almost entirely lacking in the West during at least the last hundred years. That is why we cannot trust one another; why most people live in a state of continuous anxiety; why despite all our technologies communication becomes ever more difficult; and why we need ever more organised *welfare* to plaster over the gaping holes torn by the progressive disappearance of spontaneous social cohesion. The Christian (and other) saints knew themselves so well that they could 'see' into the inside of other beings. The idea that Saint Francis could communicate with animals, birds, even flowers, must of course appear incredible to modern men who have so neglected self-knowledge that they have difficulties communicating even with their wives.

The 'inner world', seen as fields of knowledge (field one and field two), is the world of freedom; the outer world (field three and field four), the world of necessity. All our serious problems of living are suspended, as it were, between these two poles of freedom and necessity. They are divergent problems, not for solving. Our anxiety to solve problems stems from our total lack of self-knowledge, which has created the kind of existential anguish of which Kierkegaard is one of the early and most impressive exponents. The anxiety to solve problems has led to a virtually total concentration of intellectual effort on the study of *convergent* problems. Great pride is being taken in this voluntary limitation of the limitless Intellect and its confinement to 'the art of the soluble'. 'Good scientists', says Peter B. Medawar, 'study the most important problems they think they can solve. It is, after all, their professional business to solve problems, not merely to grapple with them.'[7] This is fair enough; it clearly demonstrates, at the same time, that 'good scientists' in this sense can deal only with the dead aspect of the Universe. The real problems of life have to be *grappled with*. To repeat a quotation from Thomas Aquinas, 'The slenderest knowledge that may be obtained of the highest things is more desirable than the most certain knowledge obtained of lesser things'; and 'grappling' with the help of slender knowledge is the real stuff of life, whereas solving problems—which, to be soluble, must be convergent—with the help of 'the most certain knowledge obtained of lesser things' is merely one of many useful and perfectly honourable human activities designed to save labour.

While the logical mind abhors divergent problems and tries to run away from them, the higher faculties of man accept the challenges of life as they are offered, without complaint, knowing that when things are most contradictory, absurd, difficult and frustrating, then — *just then* — life really makes sense: as a mechanism provoking and almost forcing us to develop towards higher Levels of Being. The question is one of faith, of choosing our own 'grade of significance'. Our ordinary mind always tries to persuade us that we are nothing but acorns and that our greatest happiness will be to become bigger, fatter, shinier acorns; but that is of interest only to pigs. Our faith gives us knowledge of something much better: that we can become oak trees.

What is good and what is bad? What is virtuous and what is evil? It all depends on our faith. Taking our bearings from the four Great Truths discussed in this book, and studying the interconnections between these four landmarks on our 'map', we do not find it difficult to discern what constitutes the true progress of a human being:

— His first task is to learn from society and 'tradition' and to find his temporary happiness in receiving directions from outside.

— His second task is to interiorise the knowledge he has gained, sift it, sort it out, keep the good and jettison the bad; this process may be called 'individuation', becoming self-directed.

— His third task is one that he cannot tackle until he has accomplished the first two, and for which he needs the very best help he can possibly find: it is 'dying' to oneself, to one's likes and dislikes, to all one's egocentric preoccupations. To the extent that he succeeds in this, he ceases to be directed from outside, and he also ceases to be self-directed. He has gained freedom, or, one might say, he is then God-directed. If he is a Christian, that is precisely what he would hope to be able to say.

If this is the threefold task before each human being, we can say that 'good' is what helps me and others along on this journey of liberation. I am called upon to 'love my neighbour as myself', but I cannot love him at all (except sensually or sentimentally) unless I have loved myself sufficiently to embark on the journey of development as described. How could I love and help him as long as I have to say, with St Paul: 'My own behaviour baffles me. For I find myself not doing what I really want to do but doing what I really loathe'? In order to become capable of loving and helping my neighbour as well as myself, I am called upon to 'love God', that is, strenuously and patiently to keep my mind straining and stretching towards the highest things, to Levels of Being above my own: only there is 'goodness' for me.

Epilogue

After Dante (in the *Divine Comedy*) had 'woken up' and found himself in the horrible dark wood where he had never meant to go, his good intention to make the ascent up the mountain was of no avail; he first had to descend into the Inferno to be able fully to appreciate the reality of sinfulness. Today, people who acknowledge the Inferno of *things as they really are* in the modern world are regularly denounced as 'doomwatchers', pessimists and the like. Dorothy Sayers, one of the finest commentators on Dante as well as on modern society, has this to say:

> That the *Inferno* is a picture of human society in a state of sin and corruption, everybody will readily agree. And since we are today fairly well convinced that society is in a bad way and not necessarily evolving in the direction of perfectibility, we find it easy enough to recognise the various stages by which the deep of corruption is reached. Futility; lack of a living faith; the drift into loose morality, greedy consumption, financial irresponsibility, and un-controlled bad temper; a self-opinionated and obstinate individualism; violence, sterility, and lack of reverence for life and property including one's own; the exploitation of sex, the debasing of language by advertisement and propaganda, the commercialising of religion, the pander-ing to superstition and the conditioning of people's minds by mass-hysteria and 'spell-binding' of all kinds, venality and string-pulling in public affairs, hypocrisy, dishonesty in material things, intellectual dishonesty, the fomenting of discord (class against class, nation against nation) for

what one can get out of it, the falsification and destruction of all the means of communication; the exploitation of the lowest and stupidest mass-emotions; treachery even to the fundamentals of kinship, country, the chosen friend, and the sworn allegiance: these are the all-too-recognisable stages that lead to the cold death of society and the extinguishing of all civilised relations.[1]

What an array of divergent problems! Yet people go on clamouring for 'solutions', and become angry when they are told that the restoration of society must come from within and cannot come from without. The above passage was written a quarter of a century ago. Since then, there has been further progress downhill, and the description of the *Inferno* sounds even more familiar.

But there have also been positive changes: Some people are no longer angry when told that restoration must come from within; the belief that everything is 'politics' and that radical rearrangements of 'system' will suffice to save civilisation is no longer held with the same fanaticism as it was held twenty-five years ago; everywhere in the modern world there are now experiments in New Life-Styles and Voluntary Simplicity; the arrogance of materialistic scientism is in decline, and it is sometimes tolerated even in polite society to mention God. Admittedly, some of this change of mind stems not initially from spiritual insight, but from materialistic fear aroused by the environmental crisis, the fuel crisis, the threat of a food crisis and the indications of a coming health crisis. In the face of these—and many other—threats, most people still try to believe in the 'technological fix'. If we could develop *fusion energy*, they say, our fuel problems would be solved; if we would perfect the processes of turning oil into edible proteins, the world's food problem would be solved; and the development of new drugs will surely avert any threat of a health crisis … and so on.

All the same, the faith in modern man's omnipotence is wearing thin. Even if all the 'new' problems were solved by technological fixes, the state of futility, disorder and corruption would remain. It existed before the present crises became acute, and it will not go away by itself. More and more people are beginning to realise that 'the modern experiment' has failed. It received its early impetus by what I have called the Cartesian revolution, which, with implacable logic, separated man from those Higher Levels that alone can maintain his humanity. Man closed the gates of Heaven against himself and tried, with immense energy and ingenuity, to confine himself to the Earth. He is now discovering that the Earth is but a transitory state, so that a refusal to reach for Heaven means an involuntary descent into Hell.

It may conceivably be possible to live without churches; but it is not possible to live without religion, that is without systematic work to keep in contact with and develop towards Higher Levels than those of 'ordinary life', with all its pleasure and pain, sensation and gratification, refinement or crudity— whatever it may be. *The modern experiment to live without religion has failed*, and once we have understood this, we know what our 'post-modern' tasks really are. Significantly, a large number of young people (of varying ages!) are looking in the right direction. They feel it in their bones that the ever more successful solution of convergent problems is of no help at all— it may even be a hindrance—in learning how to cope, to grapple with, the divergent problems that are the stuff of real life.

The art of living is always to make a good thing out of a bad thing. Only if we *know* that we have actually descended into infernal regions where nothing awaits us but 'the cold death of society and the extinguishing of all civilised relations', can we summon the courage and imagination needed for a 'turning around', a *metanoia*. This then leads to seeing the world in a new light, namely as a place where the things modern man continuously talks about and always fails to accomplish can actually be done. The generosity of the Earth allows us to feed all mankind; we know enough about ecology to keep the Earth a healthy place; there is enough room on the Earth, and there are enough materials, so that everybody can have adequate shelter; we are quite competent enough to produce sufficient supplies of necessities so that no one need live in misery. Above all, we shall then see that the economic problem is a convergent problem that has been solved already: we know how to provide enough, and do not require any violent, inhuman, aggressive technologies to do so. There *is* no economic problem and, in a sense, there never has been. But there is a moral problem, and moral problems are not convergent, capable of being solved so that future generations can live without effort; no, they are divergent problems, which have to be understood and transcended.

Can we rely on it that a 'turning around' will be accomplished by enough people quickly enough to save the modern world? This question is often asked, but whatever answer is given to it will mislead. The answer 'Yes' would lead to complacency; the answer 'No' to despair. It is desirable to leave these perplexities behind us and get down to work.

Notes

CHAPTER 1 On Philosophical Maps

1 To be precise, in August 1968, during the week of the Soviet invasion of Czechoslovakia.

2 St Thomas Aquinas, *Summa theologica*, I, 1, 5 ad 1.

3 Maurice Nicoll, *Psychological Commentaries* (London, 1952), vol. 1.

4 Victor E. Frankl, 'Reductionism and Nihilism', in A. Koestler and J. R. Smythies (eds), *Beyond Reductionism* (London, 1969).

5 Ibid.

6 Quoted by Michael Polanyi, *Personal Knowledge* (London, 1958).

7 Koestler and Smythies, op. cit.

8 Plato, *Symposium*, trans. Jowett (Oxford, 1871).

9 Cf. F. S. C. Northrop, *The Logic of the Sciences and Humanities* (New York, 1959).

10 W. Y. Evans-Wentz, *Tibetan Yoga and Secret Doctrines* (Oxford, 1935).

11 René Descartes, *Rules for the Direction of the Mind*, trans. Elizabeth Haldane and G. R. T. Ross. (Encyclopaedia Britannica, Chicago, 1971).

12 Ibid.

13 René Descartes, *Discourse on Method*.

14 Descartes, *Rules for the Direction of the Mind*.

15 Ibid.

16 Jacques Maritain, *The Dream of Descartes* (London, 1946).

17 Ibid.
18 Descartes, *Rules for the Direction of the Mind.*
19 Etienne Gilson, *The Unity of Philosophical Experience* (London, 1938).
20 Ibid.
21 Blaise Pascal, *Pensées*, section II, no. 169.
22 Quoted in *Great Books of the Western World. The Great Ideas* (Chicago, 1953), vol. 1, ch. 33.
23 St Thomas Aquinas, *Summa contra Gentiles*, vol. 1 (London, 1924–8).
24 St Thomas Aquinas, *Summa contra Gentiles*, vol. 3 (London, 1924–8).

CHAPTER 2 Levels of Being

1 Arthur O. Lovejoy, *The Great Chain of Being* (New York, 1960).
2 Catherine Roberts, *The Scientific Conscience* (Fontwell, Sussex, 1974).

CHAPTER 3 Progressions

1 St Thomas Aquinas, *Summa contra Gentiles*, vol. 5, book 4, ch. XI.
2 Maurice Nicoll, *Living Time* (London, 1952), ch. 1.
3 Nicoll, op. cit.

CHAPTER 4 *Adaequatio* I

1 G. N. M. Tyrrell, *Grades of Significance* (London, 1930).
2 R. L. Gregory, *Eye and Brain—the Psychology of Seeing* (London, 1966).
3 Tyrrell, op. cit.
4 Matt. XIII.13.
5 Matt. XIII.15; Acts XXVIII.27.
6 Rev. III.16.

7 Etienne Gilson, *The Christian Philosophy of Saint Augustine* (London, 1961).

8 Ibid.

9 Jalal al-Din Rumi, *Mathnawi* (Gibb Memorial Series, London, 1926–34), vol. 4.

10 John Smith the Platonist, *Select Discourses* (London, 1821).

11 Richard of Saint-Victor, *Selected Writings on Contemplation* (London, 1957).

12 *Suttanipata*, IV, ix, 3.

13 *Majjhima Nikaya*, LXX.

14 Maurice Nicoll, *Living Time* (London, 1952), ch. x.

CHAPTER 5 *Adaequatio* II

1 Sir Arthur Eddington, *The Philosophy of Physical Science* (London, 1939).

2 René Descartes, Preface to the French translation of the *Principia Philosophiae*, part II.

3 Cf. Ernst Lehrs, *Man or Matter* (London, 1951). 'In fact, physical science is essentially, as Professor Eddington put it, a "pointer reading science". Looking at this fact in our way we can say that all pointer instruments which man has constructed ever since the beginning of science, have as their model man himself, restricted to colourless, non-stereoscopic observation. For all that is left to him in this condition is to focus points in space and register changes of their positions. Indeed, the perfect scientific observer is himself the arch-pointer-instrument' (pp. 132–3).

4 René Descartes, Preface to the French translation of the *Principia Philosophiae*, part II.

5 Etienne Gilson, *The Christian Philosophy of Saint Augustine* (London, 1961).

6 Etienne Gilson, *The Unity of Philosophical Experience* (London, 1938).

7 Ibid.

8 Abraham Maslow, *The Psychology of Science* (New York, 1966), ch. 4.

9 William James, *The Will to Believe* (London, 1899).

CHAPTER 6   The Four Fields of Knowledge—
            Field One

1   Whitall N. Perry, *A Treasury of Traditional Wisdom*
    (London, 1971).

2   *Measure for Measure*, III, ii, 250; see also Beryl Pogson, *In
    the East My Pleasure Lies* (London, 1950), and Martin
    Lings, *Shakespeare in the Light of Sacred Art* (London,
    1966).

3   P. D. Ouspensky, *The Psychology of Man's Possible Evolution*,
    (London, 1951), 1st lecture.

4   Ibid.

5   Joseph Campbell, 'Prologue', *The Hero with a Thousand
    Faces* (New York, 1949).

6   Ernest Wood, *Yoga* (Harmondsworth, 1959), ch. 4.

7   Ouspensky, op. cit.

8   Nyanaponika Thera, 'Introduction', *The Heart of Buddhist
    Meditation, a Handbook of Mental Training Based on the
    Buddha's Way of Mindfulness* (London, 1962).

9   Ibid.

10 Ibid.

11 'The Instruction to Bahiya', quoted by Nyanaponika
    Thera, op. cit.

12 *The Cloud of Unknowing*, a new translation by Clifton
    Wolters (Harmondsworth, 1961).

13 *Majjhima Nikaya*, CXL. Cf. also J. Evola, *The Doctrine of
    Awakening* (London, 1951), ch. IV.

14 *The Cloud of Unknowing*, op. cit.

15 In *A Treasury of Russian Spirituality*, compiled and edited by
    G. P. Fedotov (London, 1952).

16 See *Writings from the Philokalia on Prayer of the Heart*
    (London, 1951) and *Early Fathers from the Philokalia*
    (London, 1954).

17 Hieromonk Kallistos (Timothy Ware) in his introduction
    to *The Art of Prayer* (see next note).

18 *The Art of Prayer, An Orthodox Anthology*, compiled by
    Igumen Chariton of Valamo (London, 1966), ch. III,
    iii.

19 Wilder Penfield, *The Mystery of the Mind* (Princeton,
    1975).

20 Ibid.
21 'On The Prayer of Jesus', from the *Ascetic Essays of Bishop Ignatius Brianchaninov* (London, 1952). The quotations are from the 'Introduction' by Alexander d'Agapeyeff.
22 W. T. Stace, *Mysticism and Philosophy* (London, 1961).
23 Ibid.
24 Ibid.
25 Ibid.
26 Ibid.

CHAPTER 7   The Four Fields of Knowledge—
             Field Two

1   Rom. VIII.22.
2   J. G. Bennett, *The Crisis in Human Affairs* (London, 1948), ch. 6.
3   William James, *The Principles of Psychology* (Chicago, 1952), ch. 25.
4   The Venerable Mahasi Sayadaw, *The Progress of Insight through the Stages of Purification* (Kandy, Ceylon, 1965), ch. IV, p. 4.
5   St John of the Cross, *Ascent of Mount Carmel*, book II, ch. 11, in *The Complete Works of Saint John of the Cross*, translated and edited by E. Allison Peers (London, 1935).
6   Ernest Wood, *Yoga* (Harmondsworth, 1959).
7   W. Y. Evans-Wentz, 'General Introduction', *Tibetan Yoga and Secret Doctrines* (London, 1935), section XI.
8   Ibid.
9   Ernest Wood, *Practical Yoga, Ancient and Modern* (London, 1951), ch. 4.
10 Lorber's writings are published, in German only, by Lorber-Verlag, Bietigheim, Württemberg, West Germany.
11 See books on Edgar Cayce by Hugh Lynn Cayce and Edgar Evans Cayce (his sons), Thomas Sugrue, M. E. Penny Baker, Elsie Sechrist, W. and G. McGarey, Mary Ellen Carter, Doris Agee, Noel Langley, Harmon Hartzell Bro. (New York).
12 Doris Agee, *Edgar Cayce on ESP* (New York, 1969), ch. 2.

CHAPTER 8 The Four Fields of Knowledge —
Field Three

1 Maurice Nicoll, *Psychological Commentaries on the Teaching
of G. I. Gurdjieff and P. D. Ouspensky* (London, 1952–6),
vol. 1, p. 266.
2 Ibid., vol. 4, p. 1599.
3 Ibid., vol. 1, p. 267.
4 Ibid., vol. 1, p. 259.

CHAPTER 9 The Four Fields of Knowledge —
Field Four

1 Arthur Livingston in his 'Editor's Note' to *The Mind and
Society* (see next note).
2 Vilfredo Pareto, *The Mind and Society* (London, 1935),
paragraphs 69/2; 99/100; 109/110.
3 Ibid.
4 Ibid.
5 F. S. C. Northrop, *The Logic of the Sciences and the Humanities*
(New York, 1959), ch. 8.
6 René Guénon, *Symbolism of the Cross* (London, 1958), ch. IV.
7 'Nature, Philosophy of', in *The New Encyclopaedia Britannica*
(1975), vol. 12, p. 873.
8 Ibid.
9 Karl Stern, *The Flight from Woman* (New York, 1965)
ch. 5.
10 René Descartes, *Discourse on Method*, part VI.
11 Julian Huxley, *Evolution, the Modern Synthesis* (London,
1942), ch. 2, section 7.
12 'Evolution', in *The New Encyclopaedia Britannica* (1975),
vol. 7, pp. 23 and 17.
13 Ibid.
14 Ibid.
15 Ibid.
16 Stern, op. cit., ch. 12.
17 *The Times* reports on January 24th, 1977:
Mr John Watson, head of the religious education
department of Rickmansworth School, who was dismissed for teaching the literal 'Genesis' view of

creation instead of the evolutionary view favoured in
the agreed syllabus, intends ... [to take legal action]
... Mr Watson ... was a missionary in India for 16
years and is the author of two books that put forward
the Genesis theory of creation.

A 'Monkey trial in reverse', to show that all *faiths* tend to
be intolerant!

18 'Evolution', op. cit.

19 Douglas Dewar, *The Transformist Illusion* (Murfreesboro,
Tennessee, 1957).

20 Martin Lings, in *Studies in Comparative Religion* (published
quarterly by Tomorrow Publications Ltd, Bedfont,
Middlesex, 1970), vol. 4, no. 1, p. 59.

21 Harold Saxton Burr, *Blueprint for Immortality: the Electric
Patterns of Life* (London, 1972).

22 Ibid.

23 Ibid.

CHAPTER 10 Two Types of Problem

1 René Guénon, *The Reign of Quantity and the Signs of the
Times*, translated by Lord Northbourne (London, 1953).

2 Cf. Paul Roubiczek, *Existentialism For and Against* (Cam-
bridge, 1964).

3 St Thomas Aquinas, 'Commentary on the Gospel of
Matthew V.2'.

4 Ananda K. Coomaraswamy, 'Why Exhibit Works of
Art?' *Christian and Oriental Philosophy of Art* (New York,
1956), ch. 1.

5 Dante, *The Divine Comedy*, trans. Charles Eliot Norton
(Great Books of the Western World, Encyclopaedia
Britannica, Chicago, 1952).

6 Quoted in Dorothy L. Sayers, *Further Papers on Dante*
(London, 1957), p. 54.

7 P. B. Medawar, 'Introduction', *The Art of the Soluble*
(London, 1967).

EPILOGUE

1 Dorothy L. Sayers, *Introductory Papers on Dante* (London,
1954), p. 114.

Index

SCHUMACHER'S LEGACY OF BOOKS

This is a short introduction to the range of books, essays and work left by the unique polymath Schumacher that should be of follow-up interest to the reader on particular topics. Schumacher considered *A Guide for the Perplexed* his greatest work, explaining the philosophical and whole world view underpinnings to his bestseller *Small Is Beautiful,* which emphasises the outer manifestation of Schumacher's thinking: practical solutions on a more human scale that are surprisingly inspiring and up-to-date. These first two books provide refreshingly simple but effective ideas to meet society's growing problems and are available from Vintage at www.vintage-books.co.uk

A Guide for the Perplexed gives us a holistic map to interrogate both practical and more esoteric questions throughout our lives. It meets us on a personal level, tapping into our inner heart-felt intuition which gives us our purpose and moral compass in life. It explains how society has become trapped by 'materialistic' science being the answer for all questions when it does not have the possibility of answering the most important questions of life. Hence we have a seriously 'tunnel vision' cultural imbalance that is leading to personally dissatisfying lives and a broken world environmentally. *A Guide for the Perplexed* provides us with the whole world view answers, including reconnecting with our inner values and guide through contemplation.

Small is Beautiful: Economics As If People Mattered is Schumacher's most famous and quoted work which the *Times Literary Supplement* ranked in the 100 most influential books published since World War II. It promotes the need to size solutions and organisations to the human scale wherever feasible so that people can influence their environment rather than big solutions being imposed from outside without the same checks and balances. Schumacher is right up to date in delivering a message we all need to heed, whether it be about localism in politics, deciding the size of banks that are not 'too big to fail' or preparing for Peak Oil and Climate Change.

Good Work is a book composed of several of Schumacher's papers, presentations and discussions on the practical side of doing things right, which he saw as an equal element to being well adjusted in personal values and wisdom, being well considered in relating to the circumstances of any situation and in actually doing something that would improve things. This book is a rich source of specific practical problems and the way to see them and tackle them from technological to organisational and from food to education. This makes a marvellous companion to the broader books above in illustrating deep practical issues and solutions.

His book *This I Believe* is a collection of twenty-one articles, written by Schumacher for the *Resurgence* magazine. Most of these articles have been collected into this publication by www.greenbooks.org.uk.

Lastly is the book *Schumacher on Energy* which is a collection of his earlier writings from his time in strategy for the UK National Coal Board.

These can be reviewed through the website
www.efschumacher.co.uk

A biography is available, written by Barbara Wood, 2011, *Alias Papa – a life of Fritz Schumacher* which will be reprinted by www.greenbooks.org.uk. There is a Schumacher Briefing available in 2011 also from Green Books called *Small is Beautiful in the 21st Century – The Legacy of E. F. Schumacher*. There is also a good description of his life and works by Professor Walter Moss at http://www.wisdompage.com/profileswis00.html.

Finally, visual and sound recordings from his work are available through different family member websites and some of the Schumacher Circle organisations described above. An example is *On the Edge of the Forest*. Filmed in 1977, two months before his death, it captures the essence of Schumacher's life's work: to re-kindle a non-violent and permanent way of living where progress means improving the *quality* of people's lives and living in harmony with the environment.

E. F. SCHUMACHER AND HIS LIVING LEGACY – A SHORT INTRODUCTION

Schumacher was born in Bonn in 1911 but lived his childhood in Berlin where his father was Professor of Economics. He was a Rhodes Scholar in Economics at Oxford University and Columbia University, New York. He experienced and thought about a huge range of subjects during his life: running trading businesses, fleeing political oppression, working on the land, working in banks, strategy in energy industries, advising governments, experiencing new cultures such as Buddhism and different ways of living and above all searching for better practical answers in discussion with great minds and everyday folk. He was particularly good at looking with a fresh mind to find simpler unbiased truths, a most difficult virtue in our modern media culture where there is a 'strong sell' slant on everything from goods to services, politics to religion. His personal touch and humour inspired many people in his life leading to the setting up of numerous organisations carrying on his vision:

Centre for Alternative Technology (CAT) www.cat.org.uk
Green Books www.greenbooks.co.uk
Jeevika Trust www.jeevika.org.uk
Practical Action www.practicalaction.org

New Economics Foundation www.neweconomics.org
Resurgence www.resurgence.org
Schumacher College www.schumachercollege.org.uk
Schumacher Institute www.schumacherinstitute.org.uk
Schumacher Society www.schumacher.org.uk
Soil Association www.soilassociation.org

And in the USA :
E. F. Schumacher Society www.schumachersociety.org
New Economics Institute www.neweconomicsinstitute.org

Schumacher's two main books emphasise these two lessons for change above all else from his life experiences:

1. Ensure appropriate scale and technology of solutions considering people and the planet's needs – he alerts us to the benefits of the more local over the global, leading to more appropriate solutions rather than following the unbalanced dogma of economies of scale.
2. Develop your individual understanding of inner purpose and energy to create right spirit, right perspectives/ decision and right actions – he promotes the need to listen to our inner natural intuition (without ego) to answer life's biggest questions rather than relying on a limited perspective materialistic scientism or economics.

Other resources are at www.ef-schumacher.org

THE HISTORY OF VINTAGE

The famous American publisher Alfred A. Knopf (1892–1984) founded Vintage Books in the United States in 1954 as a paperback home for the authors published by his company. Vintage was launched in the United Kingdom in 1990 and works independently from the American imprint although both are part of the international publishing group, Random House.

Vintage in the United Kingdom was initially created to publish paperback editions of books acquired by the prestigious hardback imprints in the Random House Group such as Jonathan Cape, Chatto & Windus, Hutchinson and later William Heinemann, Secker & Warburg and The Harvill Press. There are many Booker and Nobel Prize-winning authors on the Vintage list and the imprint publishes a huge variety of fiction and non-fiction. Over the years Vintage has expanded and the list now includes great authors of the past – who are published under the Vintage Classics imprint – as well as many of the most influential authors of the present.

For a full list of the books Vintage publishes, please visit our website
www.vintage-books.co.uk

For book details and other information about the classic authors we publish, please visit the Vintage Classics website
www.vintage-classics.info

www.vintage-classics.info